Access to History

Italy: Liberalism and Fascism
1870–1945

Access to History

General Editor: Keith Randell

Italy: Liberalism and Fascism 1870–1945

Mark Robson

Hodder & Stoughton

A MEMBER OF THE HODDER HEADLINE GROUP

The cover illustration shows Mussolini (Courtesy Topham).

Some other titles in the series:

France: Monarchy, Republic and Empire, 1814–70 Keith Randell	ISBN 0 340 51805 7
The Unification of Italy, 1815–70 Andrina Stiles	ISBN 0 340 51809 X
The Unification of Germany, 1815–90 Andrina Stiles	ISBN 0 340 51810 3
Russia 1815–81 Russell Sherman	ISBN 0 340 54789 8
Reaction and Revolutions: Russia 1881–1924 Michael Lynch	ISBN 0 340 53336 6
Stalin and Khrushchev: The USSR 1924–64 Michael Lynch	ISBN 0 340 53335 8
Germany: The Third Reich 1933–45 Geoff Layton	ISBN 0 340 53847 3

British Library Cataloguing in Publication Data
Robson, Mark
   Italy: liberalism and fascism 1870–1945.
   —(Access to history)
   I. Title   II. Series
   945

   ISBN 0–340–54548–8

First published 1992
Impression number   15   14   13   12   11   10   9
Year   2001   2000   1999   1998   1997

Typeset by Wearset, Boldon, Tyne and Wear
Printed in Great Britain for Hodder & Stoughton Educational, a division of Hodder Headline Plc, 338 Euston Road, London NW1 3BH
by Redwood Books, Trowbridge, Wiltshire.

Contents

Preface   1

CHAPTER 1   Introduction: The Emergence of Italy   3
1 The End of Benito Mussolini   3
2 Historiography   4
3 Unification of Italy 1815–70   6
4 Liberal Italy 1870–1915   7
5 The Collapse of Liberalism and the Rise of Fascism   8
1915–25
6 Fascism in Italy 1925–43   9
Study Guides   11

CHAPTER 2   The Liberal Monarchy 1870–1915   15
1 Background   15
2 Problems Facing the Regime   16
3 The Liberal Political System   20
4 Politics 1870–87   21
5 Politics 1887–96   24
6 New Challenges Facing the Liberal Regime   27
a) Socialists   27
b) Catholics   28
7 Politics 1896–1914   29
a) The Libyan War and the Collapse of   33
Giolittianism
8 What had Liberalism Achieved?   34
Study Guides   37

CHAPTER 3   The Rise of Fascism   42
1 Italy at War   42
2 The Legacy of the First World War   43
3 The Socialist 'Threat'   44
4 'Mutilated Victory'   45
5 Mussolini and the Birth of Fascism   46
6 Rise of Fascism 1919–21   48
7 Mussolini Seizes the Initiative: May 1921–October   52
1922
8 The March on Rome   55
Study Guides   58

CHAPTER 4   Mussolini: From Prime Minister to Dictator 1922–6   61
1 Consolidating Power   61
2 Electoral Reform   63

3 The Murder of Matteotti   65
4 Emergence of the Dictatorship   65
5 Reasons for Mussolini's Success   66
Study Guides   69

CHAPTER 5   Mussolini and the Fascist Political System   73
1 Mussolini's Aim: Personal Dictatorship   73
2 The Cult of Personality   74
3 Mussolini and Government   77
4 Mussolini and the Fascist Party   80
5 Relations between Party and State   82
6 Popular Support and Opposition   83
7 Comparison of Fascism and Nazism   84
8 Fascism and Spain   91
Study Guides   94

CHAPTER 6   Mussolini, the Economy, and Society   98
1 Mussolini's Aims   98
2 Economy   98
   a) Industry   98
   b) Agriculture   102
3 Society   103
4 How Far did Mussolini Achieve his Economic and   109
   Social Aims?
Study Guides   112

CHAPTER 7   Mussolini and the Wider World   116
1 Mussolini's Aims   116
2 Diplomacy 1922–32   117
3 German–Italian Relations 1933–5   119
4 War in Ethiopia   121
5 German–Italian Relations 1936–9   124
6 Non-belligerence, September 1939–June 1940   129
7 Italy in the Second World War   130
8 The Fall of Mussolini   131
9 Assessment   133
   Study Guides   135

CHAPTER 8   Italy since 1945: Continuity and Change   140

Study Guides   145

Chronological Table   146

Further Reading   149

Glossary   151

Index   153

Preface

To the general reader

Although the *Access to History* series has been designed with the needs of students studying the subject at higher examination levels very much in mind, it also has a great deal to offer the general reader. The main body of the text (i.e. ignoring the Study Guides at the ends of chapters) forms a readable and yet stimulating survey of a coherent topic as studied by historians. However, each author's aim has not merely been to provide a clear explanation of what happened in the past (to interest and inform): it has also been assumed that most readers wish to be stimulated into thinking further about the topic and to form opinions of their own about the significance of the events that are described and discussed (to be challenged). Thus, although no prior knowledge of the topic is expected on the reader's part, she or he is treated as an intelligent and thinking person throughout. The author tends to share ideas and possibilities with the reader, rather than passing on numbers of so-called 'historical truths'.

To the student reader

There are many ways in which the series can be used by students studying History at a higher level. It will, therefore, be worthwhile thinking about your own study strategy before you start your work on this book. Obviously, your strategy will vary depending on the aim you have in mind, and the time for study that is available to you.

If, for example, you want to acquire a general overview of the topic in the shortest possible time, the following approach will probably be the most effective:

1 Read chapter 1 and think about its contents.
2 Read the 'Making notes' section at the end of chapter 2 and decide whether it is necessary for you to read this chapter.
3 If it is, read the chapter, stopping at each heading or * to note down the main points that have been made.
4 Repeat stage 2 (and stage 3 where appropriate) for all the other chapters.

If, however, your aim is to gain a thorough grasp of the topic, taking however much time is necessary to do so, you may benefit from carrying out the same procedure with each chapter, as follows:

1 Read the chapter as fast as you can, and preferably at one sitting.
2 Study the flow diagram at the end of the chapter, ensuring that

you understand the general 'shape' of what you have just read.

3   Read the 'Making notes' section (and the 'Answering essay questions' section, if there is one) and decide what further work you need to do on the chapter. In particularly important sections of the book, this will involve reading the chapter a second time and stopping at each heading and * to think about (and to write a summary of) what you have just read.

4   Attempt the 'Source-based questions' section. It will sometimes be sufficient to think through your answers, but additional understanding will often be gained by forcing yourself to write them down.

When you have finished the main chapters of the book, study the 'Further Reading' section and decide what additional reading (if any) you will do on the topic.

This book has been designed to help make your studies both enjoyable and successful. If you can think of ways in which this could have been done more effectively, please write to tell me. In the meantime, I hope that you will gain greatly from your study of History.

Keith Randell

CHAPTER 1

Introduction: The Emergence of Italy

1 The End of Benito Mussolini

On 25 April 1945 Benito Mussolini, the Duce of Fascism, the leader of
Italy for two decades, was informed that German forces in Italy had
surrendered to the advancing British and American armies. His allies
and protectors had abandoned him to the Allies and to the vengeance of
his fellow-countrymen. Angry but defiant he declared that he and 3,000
loyal blackshirts would continue the war from the mountains of
northern Italy.

Leaving Milan with a small band of followers and accompanied by
his German SS bodyguard, he headed for the the lakeside town of Como
intending to meet up with a much larger force of loyal Fascists.
Arriving in Como on the evening of 25 April the dictator could find no
trace of these blackshirts. Mussolini moved on along the lakeside and
then heading up the mountainside to the small village of Grandola.
Here he at last found the main body of the Fascist forces. The Duce
wanted to know how many men he now had at his disposal. Receiving
no answer from the blackshirt commander he asked again,

'Well, tell me. How many?'
'Twelve', came the embarrassed reply.

Whatever illusions the Duce still had were shattered. The man who
had once boasted of possessing an army of 'eight million bayonets' and
an airforce large enough to 'blot out the sun', the leader who had once
claimed to have the support of over 95 per cent of Italians was left with
only a handful of supporters.

With all hope lost, Mussolini was persuaded to join a German convoy
heading towards the Austrian border. Donning a German helmet and
overcoat he tried to disguise himself. A few miles further on a group of
partisans – Italian anti-Fascist resistance fighters – halted the convoy
and searched it. Peering into the back of a truck a partisan spotted a
hunched figure:

'Aren't you an Italian?' he demanded.
Mussolini paused then replied 'Yes, I am an Italian.'
'Excellency', the man exclaimed 'You are here!'

Recovering himself the partisan arrested the former dictator and his
mistress, Clara Petacci, and took them to a small farmhouse.

At about 4pm on 28 April a stranger burst into Mussolini's room
calling out 'Hurry up, I've come to rescue you'. Taking them out of the

house he pushed Mussolini and his mistress into his waiting car, and drove off. After a few minutes the car stopped and the couple were ordered out. Within seconds the Duce and Clara Petacci had been shot. Their executioner was a partisan authorised by his resistance group to kill the ex-dictator.

The bodies were put back into the car and then transferred to a removal van already loaded with the corpses of 15 Fascists. Mussolini's body was slung on the top of the pile. The following day his and his mistress's bodies, now mutilated, were hung upside down from a garage roof in Milan's *Piazzale Loreto* to be mocked by jeering crowds.

Such was the ignominious end of the man who had dominated Italy for 20 years, the man who had claimed to have invented Fascism, the man who had swept away the old Liberal regime, the man who had vowed to make his country 'great, respected, and feared'.

2 Historiography

On 20 September 1870 Italian troops breached the walls of Rome and, after a brief resistance, the soldiers of the Pope surrendered. The *Risorgimento*, or Re-birth, of Italy had apparently succeeded. After centuries of division and foreign domination there now existed an Italian state covering the entire peninsula. Sixty years later the exiled Italian intellectual, G.A. Borgese, reflected

1 She (Italy) was the last born among the nations (of western Europe). Yet she had a kind of primacy, the only desirable one. No other nation, not France, not England, could be compared to her so far as the voluntary and intellectual character of her 5 foundations was concerned. She was born late, but on her birthday was adult . . . with self-knowledge and purpose.
   There was no reason for, and no possibility of making Italy the centre of the universe . . . But she might have been a beacon for all, a thing of beauty.
10   Why did it not happen?
   Why was (Liberal) Italy so short-lived?
   A course of about fifty years is less than what is ordinarily granted to the natural development of an individual life. That nation, the Italy of the *Risorgimento*, did not exceed by much the 15 duration of half a century.
   In 1922 Fascism came.

Why Fascism came to Italy is a central historiographical question. The fact that Fascism emerged first in Italy, pre-dating Hitler's Nazi regime by over 10 years, has directed further attention towards the problem.

To historians of a liberal persuasion, Fascism was an aberration, an unfortunate historical accident. The real progress of the Liberal state from 1870 – the consolidation of Italian unity, real economic growth, measured social reform, parliamentary rule – was destroyed by the shock of the First World War and its dire social and economic consequences. To such writers, the pre-Fascist regime had represented something of a 'beacon for all' in Borgese's words. The English historian, G.M. Trevelyan, writing in the years before the First World War, illustrated their view.

> Nothing is more remarkable than the stability of the Italian kingdom and the building is as safe as any in Europe. The foundations of human liberty and the foundations of social order exist there on a firm basis.

To those on the left this was sentimental nonsense. For them, Fascism was the result of the utter failure of the new Italian state. The Liberal regime had been foisted on the Italian people, made no attempt to represent or involve the masses in political life, and far from upholding political liberties, willingly employed repression against popular protest. Politics was the preserve of a wealthy elite dedicated not to the public good, but rather to the pursuit of personal power and financial gain.

This interpretation was summed up by the Marxist Antonio Gramsci, writing in the 1930s.

1 The leaders of the *Risorgimento* said they were aiming at the creation of a modern state in Italy, and they in fact produced a bastard. They aimed at stimulating the formation of an extensive and energetic ruling class and they did not succeed, at integrating
5 the people into the framework of the new state, and they did not succeed. The paltry political life from 1870–1900, the fundamental rebelliousness of the Italian popular classes, the narrow existence of a cowardly ruling stratum, they are all consequences of that failure.

Indeed, historians on the left argue that the emergence of Fascism owed much to Liberal connivance. They make much of the fact that the king, advised by leading Liberals, asked Mussolini to become prime minister and that Mussolini in his early years in power could rely on the support of most Liberals.

A radical school of historians, including the most prominent British writer on modern Italian history, Denis Mack Smith, take yet a different view. They question the Liberal view of the *Risorgimento* and unification of Italy as being a great popular national movement and instead stress how the majority of the populace were hardly touched by struggles for 'liberation' and played no part in unification. The Liberal regime, then, was the regime of a minority, a liberal-conservative elite who passionately believed and worked for Italian unity but who distrusted their own fellow countrymen. The Liberal government failed to involve the masses in the new state, but the weakness of the regime was compounded by the unco-operative attitude of the catholics, and by the revolutionary rhetoric from the left. Blame for the emergence of Fascism cannot simply be laid at the door of the Liberals.

If the cause of the collapse of the Liberals and the rise of Fascism is the central question, an associated and important question concerns the nature of Fascism. How 'new' or 'unique' was Fascism? Who were its supporters? How far did it penetrate Italian society and the economy? Why was there so little apparent protest?

This book will attempt to address these issues. It will also encourage the student to make up his or her own mind about the central problems of modern Italian history.

The following introduction is designed to provide students with an overview of the history of Italy from 1815 to 1945. It will identify the major developments and make the detailed analysis contained in subsequent chapters more comprehensible.

3 Unification of Italy 1815–70

In 1815 Italy, as the Austrian statesman Metternich pointed out, was only 'a geographical expression'. The country had not known political union for about 1,500 years. It was a collection of relatively small, often quarrelling states. In the past, notably in the fifteenth and sixteenth centuries, there had been great wealth in cities such as Florence, Venice and Rome, together with impressive cultural achievements, but the country had rarely been free from war or foreign domination. Indeed, while the likes of Leonardo da Vinci and Michaelangelo were creating their works of art during the period of the 'Italian Renaissance', Italy had been the battleground of Europe, as French and Spanish armies fought for supremacy.

In 1815 the states of the Italian peninsula were for the most part politically reactionary and economically backward. The purest reaction and the most abject poverty was to be found in the south, in the kingdom of the Two Sicilies. Central Italy was dominated by the Papal States, over which the Pope was the temporal ruler. Further north were the small states of Tuscany, Modena, Parma, and the more economically advanced kingdom of Sardinia-Piedmont, based on Turin. The traditional foreign presence was provided by Austria which occupied Lombardy and Venetia.

The period after 1815 witnessed an Italian literary and cultural revival, the *Risorgimento*, literally 'resurgence' or 're-birth', which lamented Italian divisions and foreign domination and called for the moral regeneration and political unification of the peninsula. This movement particularly affected students and the small professional classes, principally in the north. The kingdom of Piedmont was, however, the driving force behind unification. In 1859 the Piedmontese statesman, Cavour, won French support for his expansionist ambitions. French arms forced Austria to cede Lombardy to Piedmont, while Tuscany, Modena, Parma and the Papal State of the Romagna were persuaded to accept annexation. In the same year, Garibaldi, the romantic adventurer and popular hero of the unification, invaded Sicily with his 1,000 Red Shirts. Despite the small size of his army, he had succeeded in conquering the kingdom of the Two Sicilies by late 1860. Garibaldi was then persuaded to hand over the state to King Victor Emmanuel II of Piedmont. At the same time a second part of the Papal States was annexed, leaving the Pope with only the area surrounding Rome.

In 1861 the kingdom of Italy was established as a constitutional monarchy based very closely on that of Piedmont. Italian support for Prussia in the Austro-Prussian war of 1866 led to the acquisition of Venetia from Austria. Finally in 1870, Rome, the last independent territory in the peninsula, fell to Italian troops because the French had removed their soldiers from protecting the Holy City to fight in the Franco-Prussian war.

4 Liberal Italy 1870–1915

The territorial unification of the states of the Italian peninsula was thus complete by 1870. The new state was to be dominated for the next 50 years by the Liberals. Liberals believed that under the rule of educated, progressive men, such as themselves, Italy could throw off the political reaction and economic backwardness which had for too long characterised the country.

Parliamentary government from Rome would remove the local tyrannies of reactionary landlords, while the gradual introduction of state education would help break down the suffocating influence of a backward-looking Catholic Church. Economic progress together with measured social reform would free the ordinary Italian from his poverty and create a citizenry proud of its nationality and loyal to the state. Italy could finally take its rightful place alongside the great powers of Europe.

Most historians would contend that they failed to attain this vision but the extent to which the Liberal regime modernised Italy is open to argument. The period witnessed the industrialisation of northern Italy but rural poverty remained widespread particularly in the south. Illiteracy levels declined sharply in the north and in urban areas but stayed stubbornly high in the south and in the countryside. In international affairs Italy claimed great power status and joined the European alliance system, but was humiliated in her pursuit of a colonial empire in Africa, being defeated in battle by the Ethiopian army.

The political achievements of the Liberals have come under close scrutiny. In an attempt to explain the rise of Fascism historians have looked at the political stability of the Liberal regime in the years before the First World War. Did the regime manage to command the active or tacit allegiance of most Italians – acquiring an air of legitimacy – or did the regime simply represent a privileged minority reliant on a combination of force and the political backwardness of ordinary, poor Italians to maintain itself in power? Was the regime sufficiently well-established to see off the challenge of new political forces?

The 20 years after 1870 saw domestic peace and economic growth but the 1890s witnessed widespread popular protest. By the beginning of the new century liberalism was being challenged by political catholicism, socialism and nationalism. Governments tried to bring these new groups into the parliamentary system and granted near-universal male suffrage in 1912. By the summer of 1914 Italian politics was in a state of flux: a Liberal majority still existed in parliament but it was faced with a growing number of Socialist MPs and was increasingly reliant on catholics for electoral support. On the fringe of politics were the nationalists who clamoured for Italy to join the First World War. They got their way in 1915. The war was to have dire consequences for the Liberal regime and for Italy herself.

5   The Collapse of Liberalism and the Rise of Fascism 1915–25

Ten years after Italy's entry into the First World War the Liberal regime had collapsed and been replaced by a Fascist dictatorship. The central historical problem of the whole period has been to explain how Fascism, founded only in 1919 and politically insignificant until 1921, managed to destroy a political system which had lasted for 50 years. How far did the First World War and the social and economic problems it brought with it cause the collapse of Liberalism? Was the charismatic personality and political skill of the Fascist leader Benito Mussolini a crucial factor or did the collapse of the regime owe more to the incompetence and lack of resolve of the Liberals themselves?

Certainly Italy in the period 1918–22 witnessed economic depression and post-war disillusionment. The Socialists grew in strength and their strikes and revolutionary rhetoric terrified industrialists, landlords and the conservative middle classes. The Liberal governments appeared unable to cope with the country's economic problems and were accused of failing to defend Italian interests at the peace conferences. In parliament weak coalition government followed weak coalition government. By late 1921 politics was beginning to take to the streets with Fascist gangs attacking Socialists and by their action attracting increasing support from nationalists and from those fearful of a Bolshevik revolution. Mussolini, at the same time, encouraged Fascist violence and yet tried to convince conservatives that he was essentially a moderate whose dynamic new movement could crush the left and restore law and order.

By the summer of 1922 he was negotiating with leading Liberals over the terms under which the Fascists would join the government. In October Mussolini increased the pressure by bowing to the demands of his more radical followers and organising a march on Rome, ostensibly to seize power by force. Faced with this threat the Liberal regime caved in. Unable to persuade the king to sanction military force against the Fascists the government resigned. With no Liberal able or willing to form a viable administration Mussolini was appointed prime minister.

Most Italians, and certainly most leading Liberals, at the time did not see the parliamentary crisis of October 1922 as a turning point in Italian history. The new prime minister was only the head of a coalition government in which Fascists were a minority. Mussolini, though, was determined to seize complete power for himself. Over the next three years he charmed and bullied the Liberal and Catholic MPs into granting him ever wider powers supposedly to restore law and order, counter the Socialist threat, and establish strong government. Press censorship was imposed and Fascist squads arrested opponents. A new electoral law altered the voting system to ensure a Fascist majority in future elections. By the time Liberals and Catholics withdrew their support for Mussolini, after the Fascists had murdered a prominent Socialist leader, it was too late. At the end of 1925 Mussolini had made himself more than simply Prime Minister – he was Head of Government with the power to make laws without the consent of parliament. The dictatorship had been established, opposition had been rendered ineffectual. The Duce of Fascism could now begin to create a Fascist Italy.

6 Fascism in Italy 1925–43

Mussolini's principal concern was that he should remain the unchallenged leader of his nation with power concentrated in his hands. Not content with his powers to make law, control parliament, and imprison those who opposed him, the Duce encouraged a cult of personality. Noisy propaganda stressed Mussolini's supposed genius and his historic destiny to restore Italy to greatness. This incessant propaganda was to be a major feature of the Fascist regime.

Although lacking a clear policy programme, the regime did attempt to mould the life of its citizens, and set up institutions to influence all aspects of life. The corporate state was supposed to transform the organisation of industry and end the conflict between workers and employers. The *Dopolavoro* organisation was created to offer recreational pursuits of a Fascist nature to adults outside work. Nor were children to be immune from this spirit of transformation. School syllabuses were rewritten to glorify Italy and to justify the Fascist state. The *Opera Nazionale Balilla* organised youth and offered sports and para-military activities designed to encourage loyalty to the Duce, and instil discipline and a martial spirit.

For all Italians there would be new goals and a sense of mass participation in transforming the country. Life was to be a series of battles to be fought and won – most notably the Battle for Births and the Battle for Grain. Speeches, parades and newspapers were used to keep up the momentum.

Historians have noted these Fascist initiatives in domestic policy but have questioned whether Mussolini achieved his objectives. Was there a Fascist revolution transforming government, the economy, and society? How much loyalty could the regime command and who were its principal supporters? How popular was the Duce himself?

In foreign policy Mussolini declared that he wanted to make Italy 'great, respected and feared'. Mussolini hoped to dominate the Mediterranean and expand Italy's colonial empire in Africa. Constrained in the 1920s by the power of Britain and France the Duce confined himself to bluster and bullied only smaller countries such as Yugoslavia and Albania. The rise of Hitler's Germany after 1933 transformed the European situation weakening the position of the western democracies and allowing Mussolini to display his aggressive expansionist instincts. Ethiopia, then known as Abyssinia, was invaded in 1935, and Italian forces supported the Nationalists in the Spanish Civil War after 1936. The late 1930s saw Italy and Germany drawing ever closer together and contemplating war in Europe to realise their ambitions. However, when the European war did break out in September 1939, Mussolini was rather taken by surprise and lost his bravado. Informing Hitler of the lack of preparedness of his armed forces, he remained neutral until June 1940. Then, encouraged by the dramatic success of the German *blitzkrieg* against France and believing his own propaganda about the strength of Italian arms, he entered the Second World War.

Mussolini's hopes of a cheap victory soon faded. Britain did not sue for peace and on the battlefield defeat followed defeat. As the war continued and hardships for Italian civilans increased, discontent began to emerge. Finally, in 1943, with the armed forces battered and demoralised and the allies poised to invade Italy herself, Mussolini fell from power. He was expelled in a bloodless coup by leading Fascists and the military.

The new government sued for peace but this was not to end the agony for the Italian people. The Duce, rescued from prison by his German allies, reappeared as the head of a pathetic yet vicious government which controlled most of northern Italy. Dominated by his

German masters, Mussolini tried to root out anti-Fascists and anti-Nazi partisans. Northern Italy fell into a bloody civil war which ended in 1945 with the victory of the allies and the death of the Duce himself.

Making notes on 'Italy: from Liberalism to Fascism – Introduction'

This chapter does not provide a comprehensive analysis of Italian history in the period. It is intended simply to outline the major issues and provide a basic chronological framework. In short, it is an overview designed to enable the reader to 'see the wood from the trees'. Your notes on this chapter should be no more than a very brief listing of these main developments, identifying the major political issues of each section of the period.

Answering essay questions on 'Italy: Liberalism to Fascism – Introduction'

Examination questions tend to address three distinct areas of modern Italian history.

One set of questions asks the student to consider the problems facing the new Italian state in the period 1870–1915 and to assess the Liberal regime's success or failure in solving these problems. Such questions are addressed in detail in chapter 2, but you should not assume that the 'answer' can be found by reading chapter 2 alone. You may conclude from reading the chapter that Italy's problems were not solved by the Liberals but, only when you have read the whole book will you be able to assess whether Fascism or the democratic regime after 1945 were any more successful in tackling these problems. This will, in turn, affect your analysis of the success of the Liberal regime.

A second area for questions is the collapse of Liberalism and the rise of Fascism. Chapters 3 and 4 examine the period 1915–25 in detail and should be very helpful, but once again you must try to develop an overview of the whole period from 1870. Chapter 2 will help you to identify the long term factors behind the collapse of Liberalism.

The third type of question addresses the problem of Fascism itself – What was Italian Fascism? Was it a radical, even revolutionary break from the past? How deeply did it affect ordinary Italians? How much support did it command? What were the aims and significance of Mussolini's foreign policy? You may also be asked to compare and contrast Mussolini's regime with those of Hitler in Germany and

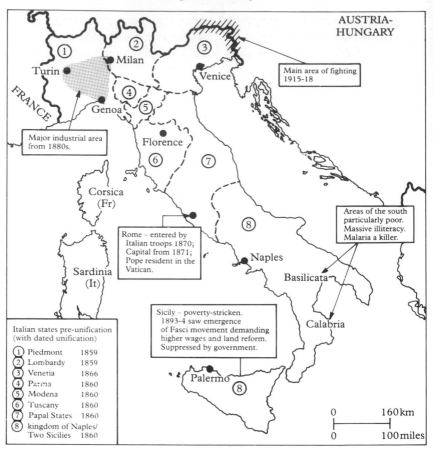

Labels on the map:

AUSTRIA-HUNGARY

Main area of fighting 1915–18

Turin

① Milan

②

③

Venice

Genoa ④ ⑤

FRANCE

Major industrial area from 1880s.

Florence

⑥   ⑦

Corsica (Fr)

Areas of the south particularly poor. Massive illiteracy. Malaria a killer.

Rome – entered by Italian troops 1870; Capital from 1871; Pope resident in the Vatican.

⑧

Naples

Sardinia (It)

Basilicata

Sicily – poverty-stricken. 1893–4 saw emergence of Fasci movement demanding higher wages and land reform. Suppressed by government.

Calabria

Italian states pre-unification (with dated unification)

① Piedmont   1859
② Lombardy   1859
③ Venetia   1866
④ Parma   1860
⑤ Modena   1860
⑥ Tuscany   1860
⑦ Papal States   1860
⑧ kingdom of Naples/ Two Sicilies 1860

Palermo ⑧

0   160 km
0   100 miles

Italy – Unification to the First World War

Franco in Spain. Chapters 5, 6, and 7 should help you to answer such questions.

As you read the rest of this book try to keep these questions in mind.

Source-based questions on 'Italy: from Liberalism to Fascism – Introduction'

1 The Views of Historians
Carefully read the three extracts on pages 4 and 5 outlining different

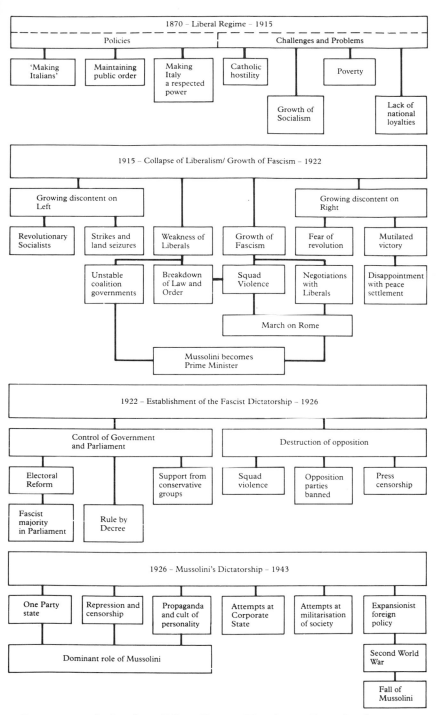

Summary – Italy: from Liberalism to Fascism – Introduction

interpretations of Italian history in the period. Answer the following questions:

a) What is Borgese's opinion of the Italy which emerged in 1870? (*4 marks*)

b) What does Borgese mean when he describes Italy as the 'last born'? (*3 marks*)

c) How far would the radical school of historians agree with Borgese's opinions? (*6 marks*)

d) Explain in your own words how Trevelyan's and Gramsci's interpretations differ. (*6 marks*)

e) Each of the three writers had a 'political axe to grind'. Explain how this fact should be taken into account when making use of such material. (6 marks)

CHAPTER 2

The Liberal Monarchy 1870–1915

1 Background

The new Italian state was a constitutional monarchy based partly on the British model. The king, Victor Emmanuel II, could appoint and dismiss the prime minister and the other ministers, but a government could only survive if it commanded a majority in parliament and consequently the king usually followed the advice of leading politicians. The kings of Italy, in any case, were principally concerned with foreign and military affairs and were reluctant to become involved too closely in the domestic political scene. Thus the governments of the kingdom of Italy were dominated by civilian politicians. These were the men of broadly liberal persuasion who were to rule Italy for the next 50 years.

However, the liberals were not a close knit group, still less a disciplined political party, but they did come from a similar background and they did share certain beliefs. Most either belonged to the small, professional classes (lawyers, doctors and university teachers) or were entrepreneurs or landowners. They believed passionately in Italian unification. Indeed, many of them had been active participants in the wars and political manoeuvrings which had brought unification about. They believed in 'progress', optimistic that in time, and through education, man would be improved and enlightened. They believed that Italy now had the opportunity to throw off her backwardness, remove her internal divisions and take her rightful place alongside the great powers of Europe.

Although they held such ideas and aspirations, most of these men were conservative by temperament. Their aim was to consolidate the unification, and thus to make the new regime safe not only from hostile foreign powers, but also from its internal enemies. To achieve this they would, in a famous contemporary phrase, have to 'make Italians'. Creating hard working, patriotic citizens, respectful of the political and social order, was possible in their view, but the task would not be easy and progress would, undoubtedly, be slow. For the moment, the masses were still too ignorant, parochial, idle and prone to riot and disorder. Above all, the masses were seemingly vulnerable to powerful forces hostile to the new regime. To the left were republicans, radicals and a few anarchists, who saw the new state as a corruption of the ideals of the *Risorgimento*, being little more than a club for the wealthy and privileged. To the right was a greater danger -- the Catholic Church. It was still an extremely powerful force in Italian society, claiming at least the nominal allegiance of the vast majority of the population, and it was bitterly resentful of the new kingdom of Italy, which had removed the Pope's independent political power. In fact, the Pope had gone as far as banning catholics from taking any part in national politics, even as voters. To Liberal statesmen the masses could, therefore, not yet be trusted to act in the cause of progress. Consequently, Liberals were determined to keep power in the hands of those who would be sure to safeguard the unification – themselves. The electorate, which numbered only half-a-million, or two per cent of the population, would be expanded only slowly, while state education would be introduced to instil patriotism and wean Italians away from what many Liberals saw as their uncritical acceptance of the dictates of a reactionary Catholic Church. Furthermore, popular protest would be viewed as subversive and would be dealt with very firmly, even if this meant using the army.

Therefore, Italian politics was to be the preserve of a minority which was wary of the population at large and was trying to cope with social change and the emergence of new political forces without altering the fundamental nature of the regime.

2 Problems Facing the Regime

The rulers of Liberal Italy had some grounds for their fear that ordinary Italians lacked any real sense of national identity or any strong allegiance towards the newly unified kingdom. To begin with, only about two per cent of the population spoke Italian. The great majority spoke dialects which were virtually unintelligible outside their local area. 'Italian' itself was simply the local dialect of Tuscany, the province centring on Florence. The king usually spoke Piedmontese.

The Liberal élite were also aware that the masses had played little part in the struggles for unification. Northern Italy had been won for the new state by the kingdom of Piedmont, helped by foreign armies and diplomacy, while the south had been conquered by Garibaldi's 1,000 'Red Shirts'. These men supposedly represented the popular elements in the unification, but, in reality, the 'Thousand' were largely students, intellectuals, and independent craftsmen. The great majority of the population, peasants in particular, were conspicuous by their absence. Furthermore, in a society where over 70 per cent were illiterate, the literature of the *Risorgimento*, extolling Italy's culture and historic destiny, can have had little effect. Therefore, it was scarcely surprising that Italians found it difficult to identify with the new state and throw off the legacy of centuries of internal division and localism. The historian, Luigi Blanchi, had attempted to sum up the situation:

1 The patriotism of the Italians is like that of the ancient Greeks, and is the love of a single town, not of a country; it is the feeling of a tribe, not of a nation. Only by foreign conquest have they ever been united. Leave them to themselves and they split into
5 fragments.

Many Italians maintained their traditional distrust of government learned under the rule of the old reactionary dynasties, notably the Bourbons in the kingdom of Naples. In fact, the practical effects of unification may have increased that mistrust. At a stroke, a region's own laws, taxes, currency, weights and measures and customs barriers, were swept away. This was certainly 'progress' from the Liberal viewpoint and undoubtedly helped economic growth in the long term, but many Italians were unsettled by these abrupt changes. This was particulary seen in the south where the incorporation of the kingdom of Naples into the new Italian state in 1861 had led to the imposition of higher taxes and military conscription. These measures, combined with economic depression, led to a large scale breakdown of law and order. Armed bands roamed the countryside, robbing and looting. Order was not restored until 1871, after the occupation of the region by 100,000 government troops.

The hostility of the Catholic Church did nothing to encourage the mass of the population to give their allegiance to the new state. The Pope, Pius IX, refused to recognise the Italian kingdom. He saw Liberalism as anti-religious and his fears were quickly confirmed by the actions of the new government. In 1861, after the incorporation of the kingdom of Naples into the new state, 66 bishops were arrested because they had not sought the king's permission before taking up their posts. The Pope responded by condemning Liberalism in his 'Syllabus of Errors' of 1864. This simply inflamed the situation and strengthened the hand of the anti-clericals. In 1866, 25,000 religious orders and religious bodies were dissolved and a new law stipulated that couples who married in church would not be legally married in the eyes of the state. For their marriage to be legally recognised they would also have to go through a civil ceremony. As far as the Pope was concerned the final straw was the occupation of Rome in 1871, and with it, the destruction of the last of the Papal States.

Many Liberals, particularly those on the right, who were more likely to be practising catholics, deplored this situation. Apart from the fear that a large section of the population might withold its allegiance from the new regime, there was also the fear that foreign powers might intervene in Italian affairs on the Pope's behalf. After all, catholic Austria already had a grudge over her loss of Venetia in 1866 and catholic France had actually garrisoned Rome until 1870 to protect the Pope from Italy. Consequently, the Italian government had sought a compromise and in 1871 had passed the Law of Guarantees. This offered the Pope a privileged position within the Italian state – he would be immune from arrest and taxation and would have his own diplomats. He would continue to occupy the Vatican and Lateran palaces in Rome, but these would be owned by the Italian state. As compensation for the loss of Rome and the Papal States, he would receive three and a quarter million lire per year.

The Pope rejected the offer. From his point of view, the kingdom of Italy was an aggressor. His authority over catholics worldwide would weaken if he were seen to be under the control of the Italian state. He was determined to have some territorial sovereignty as proof of papal independence.

Not only did the Pope reject the Law of Guarantees, he also made it clear that all faithful catholics should avoid 'legitimising' the new regime. The original instruction to catholics not to vote or stand as candidates in national elections was repeated in 1874, 1881 and 1886. Only in the 1890s did the Church dilute its opposition to Liberalism when Socialism appeared to pose an even greater threat.

The development of the national identity was also hindered by economic backwardness. The mountainous geography of the peninsula made communications difficult, but the policies of the old Italian states had exacerbated the problem. Reactionary rulers, particularly prevalent in the south, had feared the spread of new liberal or revolutionary ideas and had tried to keep their subjects isolated from such malevolent forces. Geographical isolation had been part of this policy – roads were neglected and railways discouraged. Indeed, in 1861, there were only 160km of railway track in the whole of the kingdom of Naples, and none at all on the island of Sicily. The disorders of the 1860s brought an expansion of this network, largely to ferry government troops more efficiently, but, of the 6,400km of Italian railway in 1870, only a small fraction was located in the south.

The lack of an efficient transport network in the south contributed towards its general economic underdevelopment. Italy was still predominantly an agricultural country with some 68 per cent of the population dependent on the land for at least part of their livelihood, and the poorest farming areas were in the south. The hot, dry climate, mountains, and malaria-ridden coastal plains reduced the amount of land suitable for agriculture – but the system of landholding compounded the problem. The far south was the region of *latifundia*, enormous landed estates owned by men who lived in the major towns and cities. They tended to show little interest in their lands, rejecting new agricultural methods and being content to farm in the traditional way. They employed masses of landless labourers in busy periods and layed them off when they were not required. The majority of the rural population lived in abject poverty, their plight worsened by the loss of common lands, where they had enjoyed grazing rights for their animals. This land had been sold off after unification in 1861 and had been bought up by the richer landowners.

The rest of Italian agriculture was much more productive than that of the south, but it still lagged behind the countries of northern Europe. The fertile plains of northern Italy had an increasing number of prosperous farms using modern methods, but too much land was inefficiently managed and was dedicated to the production of cereals, even where the soil and climatic conditions were far from favourable. Cereals were Italy's main crop, but productivity was low: 0.8 tonnes per hectare in the 1870s compared to 2.4 tonnes in Britain. The fact that 40 per cent of the cereals grown were consumed by the farmers themselves, indicated that much of Italian agriculture was still virtually at subsistence level. Rural poverty was to be a continuing feature of the kingdom of Italy.

Industry was also relatively undeveloped. There were few factories and those that did exist employed mainly unskilled workers, often women and children. Most industry was small scale, centring around workshops and skilled craftsmen. Heavy industry was at a disadvantage because of the lack of natural resources, principally coal and iron ore. There was some development in iron and steel and shipbuilding, but this was largely limited to military purposes and railways and was concentrated in the north. The principal industry was silk and this was also located in the north. The south presented the familiar bleak picture. Its own silk trade had been virtually wiped out by the removal of internal customs barriers. Southern silk manufacturers could no longer compete against the more efficient northern producers. Apart from small, struggling cottage industries, the only major activity was the extraction of sulphur which was used to produce sulphuric acid for the textile and chemical industries.

Unification did not bring any new investment in southern industry. The south was far from European markets, and possessed a poor quality labour force. A southerner was more likely to suffer from ill health and was less likely to be able to read and write than his or her northern counterpart. In fact, in 1871, 88 per cent of the population of the southern province of Basilicata was illiterate – over double the rate in Piedmont. That poor health was endemic in the south is suggested by the fact that malaria accounted for 20–30 per cent of all deaths in the region.

The kingdom of Italy was still a deeply divided country. Liberals were well aware of this and saw it as a real threat to the state. However, they were unsure about how much they could do to remedy the situation. They had tried and failed to reach a compromise with the Church. They were agreed that state education could foster a sense of national identity, but the problem of economic underdevelopment seemed more intractable. A programme of government investment and public works might have eased poverty, particularly in the south, but liberal philosophy was opposed to such government interference in the economy. Liberal *laissez-faire* ideas condemned high taxation and demanded prudent financial management. The state should not spend more than it collected in taxes and since the military had to be maintained and the debts incurred during unification paid off, there was very little money to spare for expensive projects. In addition, many Liberals were either unaware of the depth of poverty in the south or else viewed such squalor as the fault of idle, feckless southerners. For much of the Liberal period, poverty and the south were to be neglected issues.

3 The Liberal Political System

Parliament was the centre of Italian politics. Although the king had the power to call and dismiss parliament and to appoint and dismiss ministers, any government needed parliamentary support if it were to survive. Of the two houses of parliament, the senate and the chamber of deputies, the latter was clearly the most powerful. Government ministers were usually appointed from members of the chamber. The key debates took place there. Most importantly, deputies could withdraw their support from the government and, providing a sizeable number did so, the government would invariably collapse. These deputies were elected every five years, whereas the senators were appointed by the government for life. As the result of this the senate became little more than a retirement home for elderly servants of the Italian state. It might pass motions of no-confidence in governments but no one took much notice of them.

The parliamentary system had been partly based on the British model but in certain vital respects it was very different – there were no clearly defined political parties and there was no 'two-party' system. Politicians were drawn from the professional, wealthy middle class and represented, under the limited suffrage, this narrow social class in parliament. In Britain too it was very unusual to see men of humble origins becoming MPs but, as the electorate expanded to over 40 per cent of adult males after 1867, the parties had to make some attempt to appeal to the poorer sections of the populace. Furthermore, the British upper classes also played a major role in parliamentary politics. In contrast, the Italian aristocracy was temperamentally opposed to a parliamentary regime and followed the Pope's instruction to remain aloof from Italian politics. The urban and rural poor were, of course, disenfranchised. This left the Liberals virtually unchallenged in parliament until the 1900s. Liberals were not divided by ideology and, in fact, had relatively few major differences of opinion. Consequently, there seemed to be no necessity for formal political parties which might draw up party policy, elect party leaders, and discipline dissenting members.

In the absence of well organised parties, deputies clustered around prominent politicians and formed factions. A number of factions would agree to support each other and form a government, having decided which individuals in each faction would hold each ministerial post. Such alliances were fragile and when a leading politician felt aggrieved over an issue he would withdraw his faction's support and the government would fall. A period of political manoeuvring would then ensue, during which the various groups would attempt to form new alliances capable of commanding sufficient parliamentary support to form a new government. Deputies themselves would change factions if they were offered a sufficient incentive – often the promise of a job in government or the introduction of a bill to benefit their constituency.

In such a system politics were rarely about principles or programmes. The most successful politicians were those skilled at organising and maintaining political alliances, knowing just what to say or to offer to each faction. One of the major figures of Italian Liberal politics, Giovanni Giolitti, went so far as to compile dossiers on the weaknesses of every deputy.

To critics, this system led, at best, to ineffective government and, at worst, to corruption – the easiest way to maintain a governing coalition was to avoid tackling any contentious political issue and to hand out jobs and favours to key supporters. Critics also condemned the practice of 'fixing' general elections whereby the government-appointed prefects, the chief officials in each region, would promise state jobs and government contracts to voters. This was by no means the massive task it sounds since until the 1880s most constituencies contained only about 500 voters. Prefects might also instruct the local police to ban opposition meetings.

In contrast, supporters of the regime praised the absence of sterile political conflict in parliament. Fragile alliances did lead to a rapid turnover of governments (there were 29 changes of prime minister between 1870 and 1922) but many ministers would continue in their posts from one government to the next. Supporters claimed that the system ensured that governments could not ignore the views of ordinary deputies who, in turn, had to look after the interests of their constituencies. Above all, supporters pointed to what they saw as the regime's record of internal stability, prudent reform, and economic growth.

4 Politics 1870–87

Although the Liberals lacked ideological divisions, it was possible to distinguish – if only in broad terms – between 'conservative-liberals' and 'left-liberals'. The former were opposed to social reform and to government intervention in the economy. They were dedicated to free trade, to balancing the budget, and to the maintenance of strong armed forces. The left-liberals were prepared to consider widening the franchise, and favoured moderate social reform, particularly the provision of state education. This commitment to lay education indicated that they were more likely to be anti-clerical. They also favoured higher government expenditure on public works.

The period 1870–6 was dominated by governments of the right. They were determined to consolidate the regime. Public order was a high priority and the violence and chaos in the south was brought under control. Low public expenditure enabled the state to pay off the debts from unification. In 1876 the right proudly announced that the budget was now balanced.

The right finally fell from power in 1876 when its supporters from Tuscany turned against the government and voted with the left. The episode illustrated how fluid loyalties could be and how disputes over relatively minor issues often brought down governments in Liberal Italy. Florence, the capital of Tuscany, had been chosen as the new capital of the kingdom of Italy in 1865 and the city had promptly set about renovating public buildings and improving facilities to cater for the arrival of the national government. However, to the chagrin of the Tuscans, Florence was dropped in favour of Rome after the occupation of 1870. The enraged Tuscan deputies demanded compensation. The conservative-minded governments concerned with public expenditure were reluctant to give in to these demands. Florence extracted its revenge in 1876 when its deputies were in a position to bring down the government.

* The period 1876–87 was dominated by Agostino Depretis, who was prime minister for most of the period. This man of the moderate left proved himself expert at forming and maintaining parliamentary majorities, drawing support from both centre left and centre right. Indeed, his policy was to bring all moderate Liberals together, a goal he made clear in a speech to parliament in 1876:

> I hope my words will help bring about the fertile transformation of parties, and the unification of all shades of Liberal in Parliament.

This became known as the politics of *Trasformismo* – Depretis was prepared to accept and even invite men of conflicting opinion into government, providing they were not extremists of the left or right. He would stress what they had in common and play down their differences. This was not a cynical manoeuvre on his part to cling on to power. On the contrary, he genuinely believed that all men who valued the unification and supported the constitution of the new state, must come together in a form of national coalition government. So long as Liberals stuck together, the regime would be safe from republicans and radicals of the left and reactionary catholics on the right.

As for policies, Depretis's governments introduced compulsory and free primary education in 1877, helped the poor by abolishing the grist tax which had inflated the price of bread, and widened the franchise. After 1882, the property qualification was reduced and the age limit for the vote was lowered from 25 to 21, quadrupling the electorate from 500,000 to two million. However, Depretis maintained the literacy

See Preface for explanation of * symbol.

qualification so as to avoid granting the vote to the peasantry, a group too heavily influenced by the Church. In foreign affairs the government began by continuing the cautious policy of the early 1870s, keeping on good terms with the great powers and avoiding any conflict which might have inflamed the 'Catholic Question'. But after 1881 policy became more ambitious. In that year France seized the North African port of Tunis to the disgust of many Italians who had seen this city, opposite Sicily, as an area for future Italian colonial expansion. In the following year, Italy retaliated by joining the Triple Alliance. This guaranteed German and Austrian military support if Italy were to be attacked by France. The new state seemed to be beginning to take its rightful place amongst the great powers of Europe, and in 1885 it joined the European 'Scramble for Africa' by seizing the port of Massawa on the Red Sea coast. That Italy was becoming a major power seemed confirmed by the construction of a more powerful Italian navy. In fact, by the mid 1880s it was the second largest in Europe, surpassed only by Britain's.

The expansion of the navy also helped to create an economic boom beginning in 1881 and lasting until 1887. This period saw the 'take-off' of Italian industry, particularly in the heavy industries – iron and steel, and engineering. Iron production nearly doubled from 95,000 tonnes per annum in 1881 to 173,000 tonnes in 1887, while steel production rose from 3,600 tonnes per annum to 73,000 tonnes over the same period.

* To Depretis this must have seemed a very satisfactory record of prudent reform and economic growth, all helping to consolidate the Liberal regime. However, a growing number of politicians disliked the *Trasformismo* style of politics and deplored what they saw as the government's timidity and inaction. For them, it was only too apparent that any government which could include such a breadth of opinion would inevitably be bland and unambitious. It could only survive if it avoided tackling controversial issues. Politicians of a more radical persuasion saw the record of legislative reform as paltry. Even the introduction of free primary education had been something of a failure in their eyes – little money had been granted to local authorities to pay for new schools and teachers, and nothing was done to combat appalling truancy rates, reaching 80 per cent in areas of the south where parents needed their children to go to work. As for foreign affairs, their view was that this had also been unambitious and cowardly. France should have been resisted more aggressively over Tunis and Italian colonial policy should not have confined itself to the occupation of a worthless port on the Red Sea. The government, in short, had not looked to the future of Italy and had devoted itself to hanging on to power at all costs. Depretis himself was clearly not corrupt, but he was a corrupting influence, handing out jobs and rewards to potential supporters.

Depretis's most vocal critic was Francesco Crispi, a Sicilian, who had followed Garibaldi during the wars of unification. He condemned *Trasformismo* as 'parliamentary incest' and was determined to inject some energy and passion into Italian politics. He had no specific programme, but he did see the need for some social reform and was dedicated to making Italy 'great' in the eyes of the world. Crispi's opportunity came in July 1887 when Depretis died in office.

5 Politics 1887–96

Crispi's two periods of office, 1887–91 and 1893–6, did produce more excitement in Italian politics, but it was excitement which the new prime minister had not envisaged and did not welcome. The new era of Italian greatness did not materialise and, instead, Crispi's career ended in personal failure and national humiliation. Even the Liberal regime itself was endangered.

Crispi was unfortunate to arrive in office just as the period of economic boom was coming to an end. Growing foreign confidence in the Italian economy had increased the value of the lire relative to other currencies. This was good for the regime's ego but it hurt Italian exporters, many of whose products became too expensive to compete successfully in European markets. However, a greater threat to Italian industry and agriculture came from overseas. By the 1880s the American prairies were beginning to produce huge quantities of relatively cheap grain which then poured onto the European market. Food prices fell, hitting the profits of Italian cereal growers. Manufacturers also faced new competition in the form of cheap textiles from the Far East. Both manufacturers and landowners began to demand that the government increase tariffs on foreign imports. This would add to the price of imported goods and therefore make Italian products more competitive in Italy itself. Crispi listened to these powerful interest groups and, in 1887, raised tariffs. The duty to be paid on imported wheat almost doubled to 50 lire per tonne, and heavy duties were charged on all important manufactures, particularly steel and textiles.

These measures were designed to give the economy a respite, although at the expense of the urban poor who would not now benefit from cheaper food. In practice, the effects were disastrous. The raising of tariffs angered the French, Italy's main trading partner. Their exports to Italy were now under threat and they retaliated by raising tariffs against Italian exports. By the end of 1888 a tariff war had begun, and Italy was to be the loser. Exports to France slumped dramatically, their value falling from 444 million lire per year in the early 1880s to 165 million in 1890. Silk, wine, and citrus fruits were very badly affected. A further effect of the tariff war was that foreigners withdrew much of their investment in Italian industry, shattering business confidence. Many companies hit by falling sales collapsed because they could no longer repay bank loans. The banks, themselves feeling the effects of these bad debts, in turn found it difficult to repay their own investors. In 1893 three of the largest Italian banks went into liquidation.

The collapse of these banks not only deepened the economic depression, they also created a political scandal. One of them, the *Banca Romana*, had been granted permission to issue banknotes on behalf of the Italian state. On its collapse it became apparent that it had printed and issued a large number of banknotes illegally – in effect it had literally printed its own money, to the tune of 60 million lire, for its own use. The public outcry caused by this scandal was increased still further when it was revealed that the bank had also lent large sums of money to leading politicians. These loans had been interest free. Crispi himself had received 55,000 lire and his political opponent, Giolitti, had borrowed at least 60,000 lire. This clearly smacked of corruption.

Crispi managed to ride out the political storm and stayed in office, but the scandal destroyed what remained of his reputation as an enemy of corruption. In fact, the critic of Depretis's political methods had not only 'got his hands dirty' but had also adopted *Trasformismo* to keep himself in power. Crispi sought support from both left and right in the Chamber just as his predecessor had done. To those who condemned the Liberal regime as lacking in principle and devoted only to self-interest, Crispi's methods and the *Banca Romana* scandal provided excellent ammunition.

* The economic depression of the early 1890s not only caused bankruptcies and a political scandal, it also led to protests and public disorder. The first signs of trouble appeared in Sicily. The tariff war had hurt the island badly, cutting exports of wine and citrus fruits. Wine producers had also been affected by the arrival of a devastating plant disease, phylloxera, which destroyed vineyards. By 1893–4 the resulting hardship had combined with long-standing hostility towards wealthy landowners to create a protest movement. Workers, at first in towns but soon in the countryside as well, formed themselves into groups to demand higher wages and lower rents. These groups, known as Fasci, organised strikes and demonstrations to further their cause. The Fasci were linked together only loosely but many of them developed a vague political programme which was socialist in flavour. They called for the division of big landed estates and the end of corruption in local government, where local 'bosses' handed out jobs and decided who was eligible to pay tax and who was exempt.

Crispi's government took fright. The prime minister saw the Fasci as a revolutionary subversive movement, perhaps sponsored by the Pope and hostile foreign powers, and dedicated to destroying that Liberal regime which alone safeguarded Italian unification. In January 1894 the government ordered the dissolution of the Fasci and arrested their leaders. Sicily was placed under military rule and 40,000 government troops were despatched to restore order. The collapse of the Fasci was further assured by deporting 1,000 prominent members to the mainland.

Crispi feared that not only Sicily but the whole of Italy was on the brink of revolt. He thought he saw the enemies of Liberalism lurking everywhere. He decided that all further protest must be prevented. Socialist political groups were banned throughout the country, critical newspapers were censored, and electoral registers were altered to remove the names of all those suspected of hostility towards Liberalism.

Protest was effectively suppressed, at least in the short term, but once again Crispi was apparently acting at variance to his principles. It had been he who had criticised Depretis for not doing enough for ordinary Italians and for avoiding the question of social reform. Yet, although Crispi did pass some reforms – improving public health in an attempt to reduce the number of deaths from cholera, widening the suffrage a little in local elections, and guaranteeing the right to strike – his actions towards the Fasci and opposition groups revealed a mistrust of the masses. Crispi, like most Liberals, recognised a need for reform to improve the lives of ordinary Italians, but was determined that change should come from the top. He was prepared to discuss reform with other Liberals, but would not tolerate demands for reform from the masses outside parliament. These masses were too vulnerable to reactionary catholicism and to revolutionary socialism. Concessions in the face of popular protest would only encourage these enemies of the regime. Until Italians were 'made' in the Liberal image, strong government would be needed and political liberties could be dispensed with if the government thought that the state was in danger. This willingness to use authoritarian methods in pursuit of the 'national good' was shared by many Liberals.

* Crispi's government survived its domestic crisis but a catastrophic defeat in foreign affairs destroyed both the government and career of its leader. Crispi was concerned that the great powers of Europe, in spite of the Triple Alliance, did not take Italy seriously. He believed that the establishment of an Italian empire in Africa would increase the country's prestige abroad and would also increase public support at home. Furthermore, Britain and France were already hard at work carving up Africa between them. Why should Italy not have its share?

Massawa, (see the map on page 128), acquired in 1885, was to be the bridgehead for Italian expansion into the African interior. In 1889 a Treaty of Friendship was signed between Italy and Ethiopia in which the African state agreed that Massawa would be the principal port for Ethiopian trade. In the following year Crispi established the colony of Eritrea, based on the port of Massawa, and began the conquest of what would become Italian Somaliland. However, Italian expansion worried the Ethiopians who feared that they might become Italy's next target.

In fact, the Italians believed that the Treaty of Friendship already gave them some legal powers over Ethiopia, namely to conduct Ethiopian relations with foreign countries. The Emperor Menelik, fearing for Ethiopia's independence, effectively repudiated the Friendship Treaty in 1890, denying Italy any right to direct his country's affairs. It was clear that further Italian expansion would mean war.

Di Rudini's government, from 1891–3, was reluctant to meet the cost of such an adventure, but Crispi, on returning to office, was not to be deterred. The French were by now meddling in Ethiopian affairs, building a railway from the capital, Addis Ababa, to their colony of Djibouti. This would remove Ethiopia's reliance on Massawa for trade, and would see France replacing Italy as the dominant power in the region. Crispi was determined to avoid a repeat of the Tunis affair of 1881, where France had stolen a colony from under Italy's nose. He decided on a forward policy to intimidate Ethiopia, and in 1895 ordered Italian troops to occupy the province of Tigre. Ethiopian forces responded and an increasing number of skirmishes took place, culminating in the battle of Adowa. Here, in March 1896, an Italian army was utterly defeated leaving 5,000 Italian soldiers dead.

This was a national humiliation which was etched into the Italian consciousness and only exorcised in 1936 when Mussolini's Fascists finally destroyed Ethiopia. Crispi's career came to an abrupt end. He had tried to make Italy a great power but had seen his army lose its first major campaign, the first European forces to be defeated by an African state in modern times. His other policies had been scarcely more successful. The tariff war had severely damaged the economy and his repression of political dissent had only increased the numbers of critics and opponents of the regime. Crispi had certainly over-reacted to the dangers posed by the Fasci and socialists, but he had been correct to see these movements as new forces challenging the Liberal ascendancy. The regime would have to decide how to meet these challenges. These were to come from two sources, the socialists and the catholics.

6 New Challenges Facing the Liberal Regime

a) Socialists

The growth of socialism had been hindered by Italy's lack of industrial development and the resulting weakness of trade unionism. Heavy industry had expanded during the boom of the early 1880s, but the factory system was still in its infancy. Small to medium-sized workshops, often using outworkers, were the mainstay of Italian industry in the last quarter of the nineteenth century, and the factories that did exist in textiles and food processing tended to employ women and children. The women would leave employment to have children and the consequent high turnover of staff made it difficult to organise workers into effective unions. The real growth of trade unionism took place only after 1900 when the economy was expanding once more and new companies were emerging, notably Fiat and Olivetti, founded in 1899 and 1908 respectively. By 1902 socialist trade unions had 250,000 members and in 1908 the General Confederation of Labour (CGL) was founded to co-ordinate union activity. However, trade unionism was plagued by divisions. Solidarity was virtually impossible to achieve when some unions owed allegiance to socialism, others to catholicism, and still others to syndicalism, the belief that a general stike should be used to bring down the state and effect a revolution.

In the absence of a strong trade union movement, the formation of a socialist political party was left largely to the efforts of middle-class intellectuals. Various disorganised and disunited socialist groups had existed in the 1880s, but the first determined attempt to create a united party was made by Filippo Turati, a middle-class lawyer, when, in 1891, he organised an Italian Workers' Congress in Milan which set up a committee to arrange the founding of a new political party.

At the Genoa Congress of 1892 the movement divided into two broad groupings. The first took an anarchist-syndicalist line, dedicated to revolutionary strikes and refusing to participate in elections or parliamentary politics. The second and larger group also committed itself to workers' control of the state, but realised that this must be a long-term aim. It argued that in the meantime, and to achieve this ultimate goal, socialists should work to extract better pay and conditions from employers, and should involve themselves in local and national politics, even if this meant dealing with the hated Liberals.

This more moderate group, including Turati, became the Italian Socialist Party (PSI) in 1895. By 1897 it had 27,000 members and ran its own newspaper, *Avanti*. In 1900, it received over 200,000 votes in the general election and secured 32 seats in the chamber of deputies. According to its manifesto, these deputies were resolved to demand the introduction of universal suffrage, an eight hour day, income tax and women's rights. But despite the fact that socialism still had relatively litle support by the turn of the century and had (to the modern observer) adopted a moderate programme, its emergence had provoked great fears. Such fears were particularly pronounced in the Catholic Church.

b) The Catholics

The Catholic Church had remained hostile to the Liberal state for the first 20 years of the regime's existence. The removal of the Pope's temporal power and the state's supposed anti-clericalism were neither forgiven nor forgotten. In addition, the Church was seriously concerned by what it saw as threatening changes in society, not just in Italy, but in Europe as a whole. Industrialisation, and the consequent movement of workers into towns, threatened to reduce the Church's influence over the masses. Workers in the countryside would be more steeped in tradition, isolated from new ideas, and more likely to listen to the words of the local priest. But workers newly moved into the towns were likely to find themselves in a strange, alien society where the words of the Church appeared to have less relevance and where the voice of socialism might appear an attractive alternative. The rapid growth of the Socialist Party, the SPD, in Germany in the 1880s seemed to confirm the Church's fears. In 1891 Pope Leo XIII responded by issuing the encyclical *Rerum Novarum*. This stated the Church's position – capitalist society was unjust, but catholics should not remain aloof from this society. Instead, they should work to change it by pressing for moderate reforms and by trying to ameliorate the conditions of workers. This was a sign that catholics might now involve themselves in politics indirectly.

In Italy, although it was still reluctant to come to terms with the Liberals, the Church increasingly saw socialism as the greater danger. The vehemence of this opposition to socialism was shown by the Bishop of Verona's letter to his parishioners, written in 1901.

> Socialism is the most abject slavery, it is flagrant injustice, it is the craziest folly, it is a social crime, it is the destruction of the family and of public welfare, it is the self-proclaimed and inevitable enemy of religion, and it leads to anarchy.

More practical measures to thwart socialism were taken in 1904, when the Pope, frightened by the general strike in September of that year, permitted catholics to vote in national elections, but only in those constituencies where their abstention might allow a socialist to be elected. In 1905 bishops were given the discretion to decide whether catholics in their dioceses might vote in general elections 'to help the maintenance of social order'. By 1909 catholics had the Church's permission to vote in about 150 constituencies and were putting themselves forward as candidates for election.

The Pope was still adamantly opposed to the formation of a catholic political party which might rival his authority over the faithful, but the catholics still presented a major challenge to the Liberal regime. Now that the catholics were active participants in national politics, was it possible to ignore them, or must some form of accommodation be attempted? If there was to be a *rapprochement*, what would the terms be, and how could leading Liberals deal with the remaining anti-clericals in their own ranks?

7 Politics 1896–1914

The collapse of Crispi's government did not lead to any immediate changes in policy. Peace was made with Ethiopia, but on the domestic front repression was maintained and even increased. Dissent was subversion and concessions were signs of weakness. This policy culminated in the traumatic events of 1898. The poor harvest of 1897, combined with the high duty on imported wheat, pushed up the price of food. Street demonstrations against high prices and shortages began in the south in early 1898 and by April had spread to most parts of the country. The government imagined some hidden hand behind these popular protests. When the attempt to arrest some socialist newspaper sellers in Milan led to widespread rioting, the authorities thought that they had uncovered a socialist conspiracy. The army was brought in to suppress the riots, killing up to 200 people in the process. Martial law was declared in four provinces, all suspected subversives were arrested, and the press was heavily censored. Thousands of people were jailed on the flimsiest evidence.

The repression worked in that the protestors were silenced but the problem was not solved. Opposition did not disappear: it simply went underground. In fact, the methods used by the authorities only increased public disaffection. It became ever more clear to most Liberals that repression was not a viable long-term policy. By the beginning of the new century the voices of moderation were starting to be heard.

The most persuasive advocate of a new approach was Giovanni Giolitti, the man who was to dominate Italian politics for over a decade. Giolitti believed in Liberalism and was determined to defend the constitution, but he was also convinced that Liberals had made the mistake of ignoring the plight of ordinary Italians. Indeed, he considered that the troubles of the 1890s had been partly of the Liberals' own making. In 1900 he told parliament:

1 The country is sick politically and morally, but the principal cause of its sickness is that the classes in power have been spending enormous sums on themselves and their own interests, and have obtained the money almost entirely from the poorer
5 sections of society . . . When in the financial emergency of 1893 I had to call on the rich to make a small sacrifice, they began a rebellion (in Parliament) against the government even more effective than the contemporary revolt of the poor Sicilian peasantry, and Sonnino who took over from me had to find the
10 money by increasing still further the price of salt and the excise on cereals. I deplore as much as anyone the struggle between classes but at least let us be fair and ask who started it.

The disorders were not a temporary phenomenon to be met by force, but instead signified a fundamental change in Italian society. Giolitti told the chamber of deputies in 1901:

1 The upward movement of the popular classes is accelerating day
   by day, and is an invincible movement, because it is common to
   all civilized countries and based on the principle of the equality of
   all men. Let no one delude himself that he can prevent the
5 popular classes from conquering their share of political and
   economic influence . . . It depends chiefly on us, on the attitude
   of the constitutional parties in their relations with the popular
   classes whether the emergence of these shall be a new conservative force, or whether instead it shall be a whirlwind that will be
10 the ruin of our country's fortunes.

Continued repression, then, would only fuel the 'struggle between
classes' and create a socialist movement dedicated to revolution. The
only alternative was to demonstrate that government could be sympathetic to the demands of labour. Government should no longer be
seen as the enemy of the urban worker and the rural poor. Moderate
socialists should be encouraged to play a constructive role in parliamentary politics, even to the point of being invited to join Liberal
governments.
   * As minister of the interior from 1901–3 and then as prime minister
for all but three of the years 1903–14, Giolitti tried to put his
philosophy into action. In the field of social reform he was responsible
for the passage of legislation forcing employers to grant one rest day per
week and outlawing the employment of children under the age of 12.
Government expenditure on public works was increased, until, by
1907, the state was spending over 50 per cent more than it had done in
1900. Part of this money had gone to improving roads, farming, and the
quality of drinking water in the south. Taxes on food, which affected
the poor relatively more than the rich, were reduced and the drug
quinine was supplied free of charge to areas affected by malaria.
   Giolitti's most controversial policy addressed the issue of labour
disputes. Liberal governments recognised that workers had the right to
strike but were very often prepared to view picketing strikers as
potentially revolutionary mobs to be dispersed by the police. This was
particularly the case in the late 1890s when troops were frequently used
to intimidate strikers. Giolitti, in contrast to his predecessors, was
determined that the state should remain neutral in disputes between
employers and employees. He thought that only if the government was
seen to be neutral in strikes would workers support the Liberal state.
This new approach was illustrated most vividly in 1904 when left-wing
unions called a general strike. The strike call received widespread
support in the northern cities, but the government kept its nerve and
refused to crush the strikers. After a few days the disorganised and
unco-ordinated strike collapsed. This defeat discredited extremists on
the left, yet informed employers that they could no longer rely on the
authorities to intimidate their employees into going back to work.

Giolitti believed that employers should be prepared to negotiate with their workers. His attitude towards intransigent employers is illustrated in an exchange of letters between the prime minister and a landowner suffering from a strike of agricultural labourers. The landowner wrote:

> I want you to know that to prevent the loss of crops I am forced to labour in the fields day and night with other members of my family and friends.

The prime minister replied:

> I am happy, Signor Count, that you have taken work which can only improve your health, and which will help you to understand how hard and bitter is the life of your peasants.

To improve relations between the two sides of industry, the government encouraged the emergence of arbitrators. These arbitrators were independent officials who listened to the arguments of both employers and employees and then recommended a compromise. Employers began to be more conciliatory. Gradually, they conceded, for example, that workers could not be sacked without good cause or simply for going on strike.

* Giolitti's policy certainly won the support of many moderate socialists, particularly those who sat in the chamber of deputies. Socialist deputies were prepared to support Giolitti's government in the chamber, and effectively became part of his coalition. The prime minister also attempted to mend fences with the catholics. The continuing anti-clericalism of many Liberals, together with Giolitti's own refusal to grant concessions over the question of Rome, meant that relations with the Vatican remained frosty, but he did manage to strike up a working relationship with moderate catholic groups. These groups feared socialism, but they also distrusted more radical catholic groups who talked about creating a party dedicated to widespread social reform. They were encouraged by Giolitti's willingness to drop a proposed law permitting divorce and they began to cast their votes in favour of those Liberals willing to stand up for catholic interests, such as private Church schools. This co-operation was particularly seen in local politics where catholics voted for sympathetic liberals and even stood for election themselves. By 1911, catholics were part of the governing coalitions in big cities such as Turin, Bologna, Florence and Venice.

Giolitti's grand design of a *Trasformismo* which would bring all men of good will together to protect the state, seemed to be coming to fruition. Socialists and catholics no longer appeared to be such subversive outcasts from Liberal Italy. However, Giolitti's coalition was very fragile and was to be destroyed by the consequences of a colonial war and the introduction of universal suffrage.

a) The Libyan War and the Collapse of Giolittianism

In September 1911 Italy invaded Libya in North Africa. Giolitti hoped to defeat this outpost of the Turkish empire quickly and to establish an Italian colony there. Italy had harboured ambitions in North Africa since the early 1880s when the French seized Tunis. In 1911 France seemed to be consolidating her control of Morocco and Algeria and, it was feared, might turn her attention to Algeria's neighbour, Libya. Public opinion, whipped up by the press, would not stand for another humiliation and demanded intervention. Giolitti bowed to the pressure.

The war itself was relatively successful, certainly when compared to the Ethiopian campaign of 1896. The major Libyan towns and ports were taken within three weeks and Turkey formally ceded the territory to Italy in October 1912. Italian forces were still harried by Arab guerrilla groups, but the adventure appeared a resounding success for the Liberal government.

In the event, however, the victory helped destroy Giolitti's hopes of a grand *Trasformismo*. In the first place, the tacit alliance between moderate socialists and Giolittian Liberals collapsed. The Socialist party had condemned the war and revolutionaries displaced the moderate reformists as the dominant faction within the party. The socialist newspaper, *Avanti*, edited by a young firebrand named Benito Mussolini, now called for the abolition of private property and advocated violent strikes to overthrow the state. The right was appalled, and many blamed Giolitti's conciliatory policy towards labour. They had hated his refusal to use force against strikes and insisted that such weakness had only encouraged left-wing extremism. Such conservatives began to listen to those who condemned not just Giolitti, but the whole Liberal system. These nationalists despised the manoeuvrings in parliament, accused the politicians of neglecting Italian interests, and demanded higher defence spending and colonial expansion. Italy must be a true 'great power' and in order to achieve this some form of authoritarian state would probably be necessary. The nationalists secured few votes but their influence over conservative groups such as industrialists and landowners was out of all proportion to their numbers. Italian politics was polarising.

The difficulties faced by Giolitti-style Liberalism were increased by the widening of the suffrage in 1912. Giolitti's reward for the victorious soldiers in the Libyan campaign increased the electorate from three million to eight and a half million. Now anyone who had completed their military service could vote, as could literates at 21 years old and all men at 30 years old, whether literate or not.

In the 1913 general election, the first held under the new rules, it appeared as though nothing had changed. Of the 511 seats in the chamber, the various liberal factions controlled 318, and could count on up to 70 votes from left wing anti-clerical liberals known as radicals. Against this, the socialists could only muster 78 seats – merely an increase of four per cent on their performance in the 1909 election – and the nationalists only three seats. However, it became apparent that the liberal majority had only been achieved by arranging an electoral deal with the moderate catholics. The leader of the moderate catholic group had agreed with Giolitti that liberal candidates who promised to oppose divorce and to favour religious orders and private schools would receive catholic votes. To ensure that they held their seats, 228 liberal candidates signed a declaration that they would support such catholic interests. Giolitti secured a majority, but it was clear that in the age of universal suffrage the number of committed liberal supporters in the country would be too few to ensure future liberal majorities in the chamber. It was somewhat ironic that the Liberal government now depended on the votes of catholic groups. Dependent on catholic support and with the socialists totally opposed to co-operation, the trick of *trasformismo* was becoming impossible to perform. Proof of this came in 1914 when the staunchly anti-clerical radicals withdrew their suport from Giolitti's coalition. They had found out about the electoral deal that had been struck with the catholics and they felt that they could no longer support a government that was so apparently dependent on the old enemy, catholicism. Giolitti promptly resigned. Within months, Europe was engulfed in the First World War, a war which would severely weaken Liberalism in Italy.

8 What had Liberalism Achieved?

Contemporaries' answers to the question depended on their political persuasion. Socialists condemned the regime as a guise for capitalist exploitation of the Italian working classes. Their argument was as follows. Wages were still very low and hours were very long when compared with the rest of western Europe. Welfare benefits such as sickness and pension payments also compared unfavourably. Any improvements in the life of the Italian worker had been wrung out of a state always too willing to use the army to crush strikers and opposing political groups. The wealth of the country had been squandered on imperialist adventures in Ethiopia and Libya. Chronic poverty was still widespread. The fact that five million Italians had chosen to emigrate to the United States of America and South America in the period 1871–1915, confirmed the failure of Liberalism to address the problem of poverty let alone to solve it. For the socialists, the question was not whether the Liberal regime would collapse, but how soon, and what methods would bring it about.

    To the nationalists, on the right, the regime was equally contemptible. It had lacked the will to make Italy a major force on the European scene. Italian interests had been neglected at Tunis in 1881 and government incompetence had caused the disaster at Adowa in 1896. For nationalists, the vast emigration was also a national disgrace. These emigrants were men and women whose energy should have been employed to build up the Italian economy and fill the ranks of her armies. Liberalism, through its weakness, had only exacerbated the struggle between classes. The state had neither crushed socialism effectively, nor provided a relevant alternative creed for Italian workers to believe in. Liberalism had never instilled an Italian 'national spirit', not least because its politicians lacked all principle. They were only concerned about their own careers and private interests and they made deals with anyone who could further their selfish aims. Giolitti himself was the epitome of such a lack of belief in public service. He had allied with socialists, catholics, and radicals and had shamelessly attempted to use the government's powers to manipulate the results of general elections.

Catholics were divided over Liberalism. Many found it difficult to support a regime so intransigent over the question of the Pope's territorial rights in Rome. Furthermore, the introduction of the wider suffrage had encouraged the emergence of catholic groups dedicated to helping the poor catholic peasantry. Governments during the Giolittian era had granted monies to southern provinces to improve irrigation and the supply of drinking water but the sums had proved woefully inadequate. Poverty remained a desperate problem particularly in Sicily where 0.01 per cent of the population owned 50 per cent of the land, leaving a mass of landless peasants. From the late 1890s onwards southerners formed the majority of those 200,000 Italians emigrating overseas each year. This was proof of the seriousness of the 'southern problem'.

Catholic groups who looked towards social reform as a means of alleviating continuing poverty would form part of the Popular Party (the *Popolari*) established after the First World War and they were determined not to be absorbed into the Liberal system. For them, the Liberals represented an urban educated élite who had little interest in or understanding of the real Italy. On the other hand, the more socially conservative catholics saw the regime as infinitely preferable to socialism. Liberalism might be far from ideal, but they feared that a catholic political party in the hands of more radical reformers would be less willing than the Liberals to defend their property interests. In any case, the Pope was not yet prepared to permit the formation of a catholic political party, a potential rival to his own authority.

The Liberals, understandably, took a rather different view of events. They might feel themselves beleaguered and surrounded by unfriendly forces, but they were proud of what they had achieved. They had held Italy together for over 40 years, they had sponsored education for the masses, and had presided over the industrialisation of the country.

Education, military service and economic growth had helped to forge 'Italians' out of the masses who, for generations, had been locked in poverty and superstition, ignorant of anything outside their immediate locality. The task was not complete, and dangers from the far left and the far right had not disappeared, but most Liberals were not despondent. True, the southern problem had not been solved, but at least some attempt had been made to improve the situation, and, in any case, much of the problem was intractable. Southern landowners and politicians had thwarted plans, drawn up in 1906, to transform the landholding system by promoting an increase in the number of small tenant farmers. The common people themselves seemed work-shy, preferring to engage in criminal activities in such organisations as the Camorra in Naples. They also appeared to be too feckless to send their own children to school, preferring them to play truant. In short, the south was its own worst enemy. As for emigration, it had proved a useful safety valve for southern society in particular. Unemployment had been reduced and wages had improved because of it. Men of liberal persuasion believed that, despite all the problems, Liberal Italy had made impressive progress. A backward, barely united state had at last taken its place among the modern European powers.

With the benefit of historical hindsight it is clear that Italy in 1915 faced many problems both politically and economically – the 'southern problem' is an obvious example – but the extent to which responsibility for this situation can fairly be laid at the door of the Liberal regime is still a matter of dispute. Did Liberals make real progress towards modernising Italy or did Liberal policies hinder development and exacerbate divisions within Italian society? The regime's narrow base in Italian society left it vulnerable to attack from political extremes but was Liberalism already doomed in 1915? By 1925 Liberalism was dead but what were the causes of the collapse – was it the result of the First World War and the political, economic, and social changes it brought with it or was the regime in crisis even before the war? This question will be addressed in the next chapter but you should already be beginning to form your own opinion about the strength and achievements of the regime. The following statistics should help you to form your judgement.

Changes in Italian society 1870–1915

Population	National Income*	Income per head*
1871 – 27.0 million	1895 – 61 billion lire	1895 – 1900 lire
1881 – 28.5 million	1915 – 92 billion lire	1915 – 2500 lire
1901 – 32.5 million		
1913 – 36.0 million	* Adjusted to take account of inflation	

Industrial Production		Value of foreign trade (billions of US dollars)		
Steel			1860	1913
(million tonnes)				
Italy	Britain	Britain	2.0	7.5
		Germany	0.8	4.3
1871 – 0.1	1871 – 0.3	France	0.5	2.2
1913 – 0.93	1913 – 7.6	Italy	0.3	1.8

Society

% of population working in agriculture	% in industry
1871 – 68%	1871 – 13%
1913 – 57% (c.15% in Britain)	1913 – 23%

Deaths per 1,000 inhabitants per year

Year	northern Italy	southern Italy	Britain
1881–5	26.1	29.4	19.4
1921–5	16.0	19.6	15.0

Adult Illiteracy as % of adult population

Year	northern Italy (Piedmont)	southern Italy (Basilicata)	Britain
1871	42.3	88.0	23.0
1911	11.0	65.3	5.0

Emigration overseas (millions)

Year	Italy	Britain
1881–90	1.0	0.26
1891–1900	1.5	0.17
1901–10	3.2	0.28
1911–13	1.2	0.46

Making notes on 'The Liberal Monarchy 1870–1915'

When reading this chapter you should be thinking about the following questions: (i) What problems faced the rulers of Italy in 1870?, (ii) How far did Italian governments attempt to solve these problems and with what success?, and, (iii) Given that the Liberal regime was to collapse by 1925, can you see any signs of this collapse in the history of the period 1870–1915?

The following headings and sub-headings should provide a framework for your notes:

1.   Liberal beliefs and aims.
2.   Problems facing the regime in 1870 – lack of national identity; hostility of Catholic Church; the south and economic backwardness.
3.   The Liberal political system – what criticisms were made of it? How did Liberals defend the system?
4.   Politics 1870–1887 – the consolidation of the regime.
4.1 Depretis and the politics of '*trasformismo*'.
4.2 Critics of Depretis.
5.   Politics 1887–96.
5.1 Protest and repression.
5.2 Failure of colonial policy.
6.   New challenges facing the Liberal regime.
6.1 Socialism – attitude towards the state.
6.2 Catholicism – fear of Socialism; increasing participation in national politics.
7.   Politics 1896–1914 – the era of Giolitti.
7.1 Giolitti's policies.
7.2 Attempts to reconcile socialists and catholics to the regime.
7.3 Libyan War and the collapse of Giolittianism.
8.   What had Liberalism achieved?

Answering essay questions on 'The Liberal Monarchy'

Most essay questions require the student to address the period as a whole. It is rare for examiners to ask for a detailed analysis of a particular decade or the career of a particular statesman.

A typical question is:

1.   What problems faced Italy in 1870 and how far had these problems been solved by 1914?

This is quite straightforward providing you do not succumb to the temptation to write a narrative account of events 1870–1914. You must be analytical! A simple but effective approach would be to re-read your notes on the chapter and to give a heading to each of the problems facing the regime at the beginning of the period. Write no more than two or three sentences under each heading explaining the nature of the problem. You can then try to categorise these problems – some possible categories are 'economic', and 'political threats to the regime'. Now do the same for the problems facing Italy in 1914 but on a separate piece of paper. You should compare your two lists, noting down those problems which had increased as well as those which had either disappeared or, in your opinion, had become less serious. Why had these changes taken place? Had old problems worsened because of government action or inaction? Had problems disappeared because of government policies? You should also make a note of any new problems which had not existed in 1870 but now faced Italy in 1914. The nationalists and their demands might be one such problem, for example. Do you think that overall Italy's problems had increased or decreased? You must now decide what line of argument to pursue in your essay. Try to work out an opening sentence which sums up your argument. For example, if you have concluded that the government did very little to address the country's problems and that these problems had worsened by 1914 you should say this in your first sentence. In the remainder of your opening paragraph you should briefly mention which problems had increased and which new problems had emerged. The rest of your essay can be devoted to explaining how and why each of these problems had grown worse.

Source-based questions on 'The Liberal Monarchy 1870–1915'

1 Giolitti's philosophy and policy
Carefully read the extracts from Giolitti's speeches to Parliament (pages 30 and 31) and his letter to the landowner (page 22). Answer the following questions:
   a) In the first extract, from the year 1900, Giolitti describes Italy as 'sick politically and morally'. What events from the previous decade might have caused him to take such a view? (*6 marks*)
   b) What did Giolitti mean when he talked of the 'upward movement of the popular classes' (second extract)? (*4 marks*)
   c) Who were the 'constitutional parties' described in the second extract? (*3 marks*)
   d) How far do the three extracts help to explain why Giolitti became intensely disliked by many Italian conservatives? (*4 marks*)
   e) To what extent did Giolitti succeed in reducing the 'struggle between classes'? (*8 marks*)

2 Economy and Society 1870–1915
Carefully examine the statistics on changes in the Italian economy and society on pages 36 and 37. Answer the following questions:
   a) Which of the following statements are supported by the statistics? Explain your answers.
      – By 1913 Italy had transformed itself into an industrial society.
      – The 'Southern Problem' was not solved during the period.
      – The provision of state education had dramatically reduced illiteracy rates. (*6 marks*)

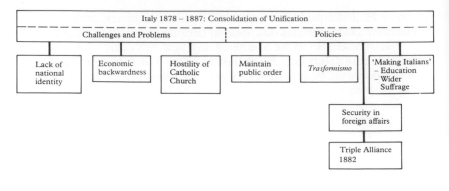

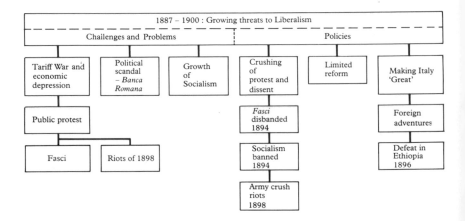

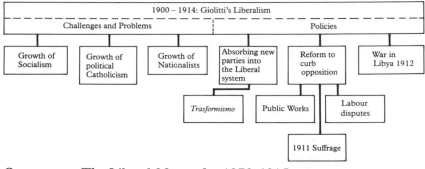

Summary – The Liberal Monarchy 1870-1915

b) Why had death rates declined? (*5 marks*)
c) How far do the statistics suggest that Liberal Italy had made good progress in the period 1870–1915? (*8 marks*)
d) What questions should an historian ask about the evidence when examining such statistics? (*6 marks*)

CHAPTER 3

The Rise of Fascism

1 Italy at War

In August 1914 the great powers of Europe went to war. However, Italy remained aloof. Her membership of the Triple Alliance apparently committed her to support Germany and Austria-Hungary but the government in Rome now declared the Alliance defunct. It was claimed that Austria had broken the terms of the treaty by attacking Serbia without consulting Italy, and by seeking to expand her empire into the Balkans.

The great majority of Italians welcomed this decision. They saw little to be gained from fighting on the side of Austria-Hungary, a country which occupied territories inhabited by Italian-speakers, notably the Trentino and Istria (see the map on page 57).

If most Italians were satisfied with neutrality, many Liberals still had misgivings. They feared that victory for Germany and Austria-Hungary would leave their country prey to powers angry at Italy's betrayal. Alternatively, if the Entente powers (Britain, France, and Russia) won, they would not be sympathetic to Italian ambitions in the Mediterranean if Italy had done nothing to bring about their victory. The government increasingly took the view that Italy must intervene in the war at some point and should negotiate with both sides in order to obtain the best terms for joining either the Alliance or the Entente. This policy was encouraged by the noisy demands of the nationalist press that Italy must grasp its chance to become a great power.

Throughout the early months of 1915 negotiations continued. It became very apparent that, although Austria-Hungary would make some territorial concessions, these would not include the Italian-speaking areas of the Trentino or the city of Trieste. In contrast, the Entente promised Italy that she would receive not only the Trentino and Trieste but also other Austrian lands in the southern Tyrol, Istria, and Dalmatia (see the map on page 57). The Italian kingdom would then dominate the Adriatic Sea. Therefore it was not surprising that in May 1915 the government entered the First World War on the side of the Entente. It was a fateful decision. The war was to have traumatic consequences for Italy's society, economy, and political system.

Although the decision to join the war was hailed by crowds of ecstatic nationalists, Italian intervention did not fire the imagination of the mass of the population. It was hard, for example, for a poor southerner to be enthusiastic about fighting for a few Italian-speaking areas on the country's north-eastern frontier. Catholics were made aware that, although their Church was broadly supportive of the war effort, it would not actively denounce the enemy, catholic Austria. Italian

Socialists openly condemned the conflict as a capitalist or 'bosses' war. Even some Liberals grouped around Giolitti attacked the decision to go to war.

Despite the absence of anything resembling war hysteria, five million men eventually served in the army, mainly as conscripts. The great majority fought bravely, endured appalling conditions in the front-line, and tolerated miserable rations and derisory pay. However, the expected victory did not materialise and, dogged by unimaginative leadership, the Italian army found itself in a murderous war of attrition. Casualties were heavy. On many occasions, thousands of lives were sacrificed in an attempt to gain a few hundred metres of mountainside.

Eventually, after two years of war, the Italian army cracked under a surprise Austro-German attack. At the battle of Caporetto 700,000 Italians retreated in disorder for over 100 miles until the line was held at the river Piave. Around 300,000 Italians were taken prisoner. Recriminations abounded. Cadorna, the army's commander-in-chief, blamed the defeat on the supposed cowardice of the troops. He executed several thousand as retribution. Nationalists blamed the government for inefficiency in running the war and in supplying the troops. The government blamed Cadorna himself, and promptly sacked him. Despite the arguments, the situation stabilised. As 1918 wore on, a shortage of food and war materiel combined with general war-weariness to weaken the resolve of Austria-Hungary and Germany. In October, as Germany reeled from an Anglo-French offensive, the Italian army attacked the Austrians. In the fighting which ensued, casualties were heavy on both sides, with the Italians losing nearly 40,000 men killed or wounded. Finally, the Austrian will to resist collapsed and the Italian forces found themselves in possession of about 500,000 prisoners of war. The victory, to be known as the battle of Vittorio Veneto, caused Austria to sue for peace. An armistice was signed on 3 November 1918.

2 The Legacy of the First World War

The war ended with Caporetto avenged and the country looking forward to enjoying the fruits of victory. However, Italians were to be disappointed. The war had enhanced their country's claims to great power status, but the eagerly anticipated territorial gains would not materialise. Furthermore, the war had left Italy with severe domestic problems which would widen existing social and political divisions.

Firstly, the cost of the war had been enormous. 650,000 men had died and one million more had been seriously wounded. The financial cost of keeping the soldiers armed and fed had placed a heavy burden on the Italian treasury. Huge sums had been borrowed from Britain and the United States of America – the national debt had increased from 16 billion lire in 1914 to 85 billion lire in 1919. However, these borrowings had proved inadequate to pay for the war and the government had resorted to printing money. This had a dramatic effect. Inflation spiralled as ever greater quantities of paper money chased ever scarcer goods. Prices quadrupled during the war years.

Inflation destroyed savings, hitting the middle classes in particular. Landowners relying on rents and state employees whose wages did not keep up with increasing prices also suffered. Nor did factory workers escape. The purchasing power of their wages fell by about 25 per cent between 1915 and 1918. Industrialists, in contrast, did well out of the war. Providing their production was linked to the war effort, they were assured of a market. As inflation increased they simply raised their prices and a government desperate for military victory continued to buy their products. Large companies such as Pirelli tyres and Montecatini chemicals made huge profits while Fiat expanded to the point where it became the largest manufacturer of commercial vehicles in Europe in 1918. However, victory meant the end of easy profits. There was no longer any need for enormous quantities of rifles, artillery, trucks and the like. A government which, in 1918, had spent 23.3 billion lire more than it had collected in taxes could no longer afford to hand out lucrative contracts. Profits fell as government spending was cut back. Hard times lay ahead for industry.

* To make matters worse, as far as the industrialists were concerned, the end of the war led to a wave of labour militancy. War-time discipline in the factories, enforced by the military, was relaxed. Workers who had resented the longer hours, the fall in real wages caused by inflation, and the ban on industrial action, vented their frustration. During 1919 over 1 million workers took part in strikes and the membership of socialist trade unions shot up from a quarter of a million in 1918 to two million in 1920.

Into this deteriorating economic situation were plunged the soldiers returning from the war. The hoped-for prosperity was nowhere to be found. Industries whose profits were falling were unlikely to be taking on new workers. Unemployment was rising and broke the two million mark during 1919. To the soldiers this seemed a very poor reward for their sacrifices.

3 The Socialist 'Threat'

As the economy worsened political divisions widened. The indusrial workers flocked to the Socialist Party, whose membership rose from about 50,000 in 1914 to about 200,000 by 1919. The party had long abandoned that commitment to gradual reform which Giolitti had tried to encourage during the pre-war years, and now advocated revolution. Inspired by the Russian Revolution of 1917, Socialists called for the overthrow of the Liberal state. The goal, according to the party, was a 'socialist republic' and the 'dictatorship of the proletariat'. The 1919 congress made plain that to achieve this 'the proletariat must have recourse to the use of violence for the conquest of power over the bourgeoisie'. Such extreme talk did not deter the voters. On the contrary, in the elections of November 1919, the first to be held under universal manhood suffrage, the Socialists swept through the northern cities, securing 32.4 per cent of the national vote and winning 156 seats. The party dedicated to revolution was now the largest single group in the Italian parliament.

The middle classes and all those of conservative persuasion were terrified. Their fears seemed confirmed when the new Socialist deputies interrupted the king's speech in the chamber, shouting 'long live the socialist republic', and then marched out singing the socialist anthem, the Red Flag. Although this was empty posturing on the part of the Socialists – they had devoted no real thought to the question of how to bring about their revolution – many people saw only the revolutionary image, not the disorganised reality of socialism. For such people a 'Bolshevik' seizure of power seemed imminent and, to their disgust, the government appeared to be doing nothing to meet the threat. Instead of using the power of the state to crush strikes and to harass Socialists, Nitti's government was urging industrialists to make concessions to workers. Shopkeepers had been alienated in June 1919 by what they saw as a government surrender to rioters who were protesting against the spiralling price of food. The government had set up food committees which had requisitioned supplies and set prices. The continuing inflation that had provoked the food riots was taken to be proof of government incompetence.

In addition, landowners were appalled by the government's failure to halt the spread of revolution to the countryside. Here many peasants were occupying uncultivated land and farming it for themselves. Agricultural labourers were joining socialist trade unions in ever greater numbers, particularly in the provinces of Emilia and Romagna, and were beginning to demand higher wages and guaranteed employment.

4 'Mutilated Victory'

It was not only over the issue of the supposed 'socialist threat' that the right condemned the government. Nationalists, who had always considered the Liberals weak and incompetent at running the war, were now convinced that the government would fail to defend Italian interests at the peace conference. They demanded that Italy should receive not only those territories agreed with the Entente in 1915, (southern Tyrol, Trentino, Istria, and parts of Dalmatia), but should also be given the city of Fiume on the border of Istria (see the map on page 57). When Britain and the United States of America refused to hand over Fiume, on the grounds that, despite its large Italian population, it was vital to the economy of the new Yugoslav state, the Nationalists blamed Liberal weakness. When, in addition, it became apparent that Italy would be denied Dalmatia because so few Italians lived there, and would not share in the division of German colonies in Africa, nationalists were outraged. To them, Italy had been cheated. Her sacrifices had won only a 'mutilated victory', and Liberalism was the culprit!

Demobilised soldiers, struggling to adjust to civilian society and with work difficult to find, saw the peace settlement as a further humiliation. Many ex-officers, in particular, feared that the vibrant, expansionist Italy they had fought for was being undermined by a weak government. Their Italy was falling into the hands of socialist revolutionaries who had done their best to sabotage the war effort. For such men, Liberalism and the parliamentary system had proved abject failures. A powerful, dynamic Italy would have to be achieved by other methods.

* In September 1919 the nationalist intellectual Gabriele D'Annunzio led 2,000 armed men into the city of Fiume and occupied it in defiance of the Italian government. Nationalists and many ex-soldiers hailed him as the embodiment of the Italy they wanted to create. D'Annunzio had shown that the way to achieve results was not to indulge in months of talking and negotiations, but rather to act decisively and not to be afraid to use force. Critics of the Liberal regime noted with satisfaction that the government lacked the will and the courage to despatch troops to end the occupation.

For over a year the flamboyant D'Annunzio ruled Fiume, holding frequent parades during which his armed supporters strutted through the streets, and drawing up fantastical constitutions for the city. He became a public hero throughout Italy. His dramatic style, his eye for publicity, and his high-volume denunciation of the government also made him something of a model for another enemy of Liberalism, Benito Mussolini. This ambitious journalist and politician, the leader of an insignificant political party when D'Annunzio marched into Fiume, was to become the first Fascist prime minister of Italy, and, by 1925, would be the country's dictator.

5 Mussolini and the Birth of Fascism

Benito Mussolini, 36 years old in 1919, already had a chequered career behind him. He had been born in the small town of Predappio in the Romagna, the son of a devout catholic schoolmistress and of a blacksmith with revolutionary views. He had not excelled at school, being noted more for his overbearing manner and bullying nature than for his academic prowess. When he left school Mussolini took a succession of minor teaching posts in village schools, but he showed little interest in his work.

In 1902 Mussolini left for Switzerland where he lived in poverty, doing only odd-jobs. However, he read widely and within a year was preaching the need for violent revolution. He returned to Italy in 1904 and took up journalism. His articles condemned the Church and advocated class struggle. By 1910 he was editing a small socialist weekly paper in the town of Forli, in his home province. A year later he was jailed for attempting to stir up an insurrection against the war in Libya. His exploits helped him move up through the ranks of the Socialist Party and, on his release from prison in 1912, he was appointed editor of *Avanti*, the party's newspaper. His journalism was aggressive and vitriolic, condoning the use of violence and condemning the Liberal state and those reformist Socialists who wanted to co-operate with it. He made it plain that revolution was the only policy for the Socialist Party to pursue.

★ The outbreak of the First World War was to alter Mussolini's career dramatically. His Socialist Party condemned the war as an imperialistic struggle fought at the expense of the working classes of Europe, and demanded that Italy remain neutral. But Mussolini saw the conflict as an event which would shake society to its foundations and bring revolution closer. By November 1914 he had resigned from *Avanti* and had set up a new paper, *Il Popolo d'Italia* (The People of Italy). The paper claimed to be socialist but it campaigned for Italian entry into the war. Mussolini, now expelled from the Socialist Party, accepted financial support from companies, such as Fiat, which would gain from armaments contracts in the event of war. His journalism helped to provoke rioting in May 1915 in favour of intervention, and he was later to claim, without justification, that these public disorders had pushed a reluctant government into war.

Mussolini was conscripted into the army in September 1915, but reached only the rank of corporal. In 1917 an accident during a training exercise caused him to be invalided out of the army, and he took over the editorship of *Il Popolo* once again. He blamed government defeatism and incompetence for the disaster of Caporetto, and claimed that Italy now needed a dictator who would direct the war effort with real energy. Although he did not yet say it publicly, he believed that he was the man for such a role. Throughout 1918 his paper sought to create a new political movement which would promote both nationalism and social reform. He was trying to appeal to the soldiers who had no wish to return to rural and urban poverty once the war was over. In July 1918 he ceased to claim that *Il Popolo* was socialist and instead stated that it was the 'newspaper of combatants and producers'.

★ Mussolini believed that it was time to translate his rhetoric into action. Accordingly, in March 1919, he called the inaugural meeting of a new movement, the *Fasci di Combattimento*, or 'Combat Group'. Only about 100 people came to Milan for the meeting. They represented a wide range of political views, including nationalists, republicans, anarchists, and radical poets and painters. They had little in common except a hatred of the Liberal State and a contempt for the class struggle rhetoric of the socialists. Nevertheless, they did manage to draw up a political programme which contained both demands for an expansionist Italy and the following, leftist, statements of intent:

1   1 A new National Assembly . . . (will be set up).
2 Proclamation of the Italian Republic.
4 Abolition of all titles of nobility.
9 Suppression of incorporated joint stock companies, industrial or
5 financial. Suppression of all speculation by banks and stock exchanges.
10 Control and taxation of private wealth. Confiscation of unproductive income.
12 Reorganisation of production on a co-operative basis and direct
10 participation of the workers in the profits.

However, the early Fascist movement lacked the cohesion to form a disciplined political party. Indeed, when D'Annunzio occupied Fiume in late 1919, it was just another tiny grouping of radical agitators. What prominence Mussolini did have was due not to his self-proclaimed position as leader of Fascism but rather was the result of his aggressive journalism in *Il Popolo d'Italia*. The proof of his movement's failure seemed to come in the general election of November 1919. Not only did Mussolini himself fail to become a deputy, polling only 5,000 out of the 270,000 votes cast in Milan, but Fascism performed dismally everywhere. Not a single seat was won in the new parliament and by the end of the year there were perhaps only 4,000 Fascist supporters in the whole of Italy. The movement appeared doomed. However, Mussolini was to be saved by the government's failure to convince conservative Italians that it could deal with the supposed socialist threat. From near oblivion in December 1919, the Fascists became, within the space of one year, a powerful force on the political scene.

6 Rise of Fascism 1919–21

The elections of November 1919 had disappointed Mussolini but had also caused great difficulties for the Liberal government. Liberals and their allies could muster only about 180 seats and they still lacked cohesion and party discipline. The Chamber of Deputies, designed to protect and promote Liberalism, now contained a revolutionary Socialist Party holding 156 seats, and the Catholic Popular Party, the PPI, with 100 seats. The Liberal government led by the moderate Nitti did survive but it relied on support from Catholic deputies to maintain its fragile majority.

  * The PPI, or *Popolari* as it was known, had been founded in January 1919, when the Pope had finally lifted his ban on the formation of such a catholic party. The *Popolari*, led by the Sicilian priest Don Sturzo, contained both conservative catholics and catholics determined to

improve the lot of the peasantry. This was an uneasy coalition which found it easier to agree on what it opposed than to devise a coherent policy programme. It was reluctant to play a major role in government but it was prepared to give its support to Liberal governments in return for concessions on policy. Despite this, the PPI remained deeply suspicious of Liberalism and did not forget the Liberals' traditional anti-clericalism.

* Nitti's government was discredited by Fiume in the eyes of much of the public and was disliked by both the left and the right, for its unwillingness either to grant major reform or to crush protest. It struggled on until June 1920. But, with *Popolari* support waning, Nitti's fragile majority was unsustainable and he quietly resigned. He was replaced by Giovanni Giolitti. Once again the great exponent of *trasformismo* attempted to appeal to both left and right, speaking of workers' entitlement to some say in management and at the same time planning to reduce the food subsidies which benefited the poor. Liberals, Radicals, *Popolari* and even a handful of moderate Socialists joined his new coalition, but the majority Socialists were implacably hostile. Although he was an anti-clerical, the new prime minister, like his predecessor, found himself reliant on catholic support in the chamber to keep his government in power.

Events outside parliament were to weaken Giolitti's government further. In September 1920 engineering workers, engaged in a dispute over wages, occupied their factories to prevent employers from locking them out. Within days, 400,000 workers from the northern cities were involved. The employers demanded that the government intervene to crush the occupation. However, Giolitti followed the policy of neutrality he had adopted in pre-war industrial disputes and stood aloof. He was convinced that the use of force would lead to a bloodbath, and believed that the occupation would soon collapse of its own accord. This policy enraged industrialists, particularly when the prime minister urged them to make concessions to the strikers. When it became apparent that a number of factories were being used to produce weapons for the strikers, conservatives feared that the revolution was now at hand. Again, in their eyes, the government was failing to do its duty. Even though the occupation was disorganised and collapsed within one month, as Giolitti had predicted, employers and conservatives did not forgive him for what they saw as his complacency and cowardice.

In the countryside, landowners were also complaining bitterly about a socialist threat. Agrarian strikes and land occupations were continuing to increase. In Emilia, the Po valley, Umbria, and Tuscany socialist trade unions were beginning to establish a stranglehold over agricultural employment. In Emilia the unions demanded higher wages for agricultural labourers and guarantees that workers would not be laid-off during quiet times of the year. Around Ferrara and Bologna no labourer could get a job except through a labour exchange run by the Socialist Labourers' Union. If landowners resisted the trade unions' demands, their estates would face disruption and their farm managers might be subject to physical attack.

The power of the socialists was shown not only in agricultural disputes but also in local elections held in late 1920. The Socialists found themselves in control of 26 of the country's 69 provinces – mainly those located in north and central Italy. The urban middle classes feared that the Socialists would now raise local taxes against the better-off. Shopkeepers were concerned about the potential competition from the spread of Socialist-sponsored co-operative shops.

* Landowners and conservatives felt themselves an embattled class. Their political enemies and social inferiors seemed to be in ascendancy and they thought they had been abandoned by the government. This sense of abandonment was intensified by the government's decision to grant permanent tenure to illegal land occupiers. By the end of 1920 the right in the provinces of northern and central Italy began to fight back. Desperate measures, including the use of violence, appeared justified in the face of revolution. In Emilia and Tuscany, in particular, frightened landowners and middle-class townsfolk began to turn to local Fascist groups who shared their hatred of socialism and needed little encouragement to attack Socialists. These Fascist squads were often small and lacking in any coherent idealogy, but they proved adept at burning down Socialist offices and beating up trade unionists. Their enemies might also find themselves being forced to drink litres of castor oil!

In their early days the Fascist squads consisted mainly of demobilised army officers and NCOs, together with middle-class students. But, as they proved their ability to intimidate the Socialists, the squads began to attract new followers. Many of the recruits were small farmers, farm managers, and share-croppers who, although far from rich, comprised the better-off peasantry. They were likely to be ambitious and anxious to buy their own land. Socialist talk of higher wage rates and collectivisation of land was anathema to them. The violence continued through the winter and spring of 1921, leaving 200 dead and 800 wounded in its wake. By spring, Emilia and Tuscany had become strongholds of the Fascist squads. The police had looked the other way as *squadrismo* had crushed the Socialist power in these provinces.

Local Fascist leaders, such as the young and aggressive ex-army officer Italo Balbo in Ferrara and the equally callous Dino Grandi in Bologna, built up their own power. Mussolini had not been the guiding hand behind the Fascist violence but he soon saw the political opportunities *squadrismo* offered. He strove to put himself at the forefront of this *squadrismo* by reasserting his claim to be the sole and undisputed leader of the movement. There was reluctance on the part of the *Ras* (the local leaders) to surrender their independence but Mussolini seems to have been able to convince even the most ambitious of them that their success depended on his leadership. His was the dominant personality in the Fascist movement and his newspaper could publicise Fascist activities. He argued that, without his leadership, Fascism would lack all coherence as the various factions would fall out among themselves. With Mussolini as leader, Fascism could be presented as a national movement with a vision of a new Italy. Mussolini, the journalist, could depict Fascist violence not as simple thuggery but rather as a painful necessity if Italy was to be saved from bolshevism. *Squadrismo* would be viewed as an anti-socialist crusade. In his speech to the Fascists of Bologna in April 1921 Mussolini tried to create this crusading image.

1　We Fascists have a clear programme: we must move on led by a
　　pillar of fire, because we are slandered and not understood. And,
　　however much violence may be deplored, it is evident that we, in
　　order to make our ideas understood, must beat refractory skulls
5　with resounding blows . . . But we do not make a school, a
　　system or, worse still, an aesthetic of violence. We are violent
　　because it is necessary to be so. But I tell you at once that this
　　necessary violence on the part of the Fascisti must have a
　　character and style of its own, definitely aristocratic, or, if you
10　prefer, surgical.
　　　Our punitive expeditions, all those acts of violence which figure
　　in the papers, must always have the character of the just retort
　　and legitimate reprisal; because we are the first to recognise that it
　　is sad, after having fought the external enemy, to have to fight the
15　enemy within . . . The Socialists had formed a State within a
　　State . . . [and] this State is more tyrannical, illiberal and
　　overbearing than the old one; and for this reason that which we
　　are causing today is a revolution to break up the Bolshevist State,
　　while waiting to settle our account with the Liberal State which
20　remains.

★ While thus justifying and encouraging violent *squadrismo*, Mussolini was also careful to suggest to Liberal politicians that all this talk of violence and revolution might be little more than bluster. Giolitti was keen to see Fascism as just another political force which could be absorbed into the Liberal system and Mussolini did his best to encourage this belief. Persuaded that the self-styled leader of Fascism was more an opportunist than an extremist, Giolitti offered an electoral alliance which he hoped would produce an anti-socialist governing coalition. Fascists and Giolittian Liberals co-operated during the general election held in May 1921. But despite this new air of respectability, the Fascist squads continued their work, killing about 100 Socialist sympathisers during the election campaign. Again, the police tended to turn a blind eye – this was what the 'bolshevists' deserved! However, the election results proved that the violence and intimidation had not deterred the voters. The Socialists remained the largest party in the chamber, holding 123 seats, followed by the *Popolari* with 107. If Giolitti was disappointed that the Socialist vote had held up, Mussolini was satisfied with the progress that his party had made. The Fascists had secured 7 per cent of the total vote and had won 35 seats. Mussolini himself was now a deputy.

7 Mussolini Seizes the Initiative: May 1921–October 1922

The elections had given Mussolini what he wanted: both an air of respectability and a foothold in parliament. He had no wish to be absorbed into Liberalism, to be a junior partner in a coalition, as Giolitti had intended. Consequently, he announced that the Fascists would not, after all, support Giolitti's government. He now saw the possibility of achieving real power. He had no master-plan but he was an extremely astute politician. He knew that he needed to demonstrate to the Italian public, to industrialists, landowners and the middle classes in particular, that Liberalism was finished as a political move-ment. Unstable, short-lived governments unable to maintain law and order or to deal with the country's economic problems would provide proof of this. He also had to convince these crucial groups in society that only Fascism could stop the Socialists and restore order and discipline to Italian society. Furthermore, he realised that for Fascism to become acceptable to the middle classes and conservatives it must either abandon or play down any remaining ideas about radical economic and social reform. During 1921 and 1922 Mussolini skilfully took advantage of his opportunities to create such an impression.

Governments following the elections of May 1921 were unstable, although this was only partly the result of Fascist actions. Giolitti did manage to form a coalition without Mussolini but it collapsed within a month. The *Popolari* had withdrawn its support when Giolitti proposed to introduce a tax which would have had the side-effect of hitting the Vatican's financial investments. Without the tacit support of this catholic party it was now virtually impossible for any government to survive, yet the *Popolari* was suspicious of the anti-clerical traditions of Liberalism and was willing to destroy any government which offended it. To make matters worse, the Liberals were divided amongst them-selves. Liberalism was still plagued by factions centred on prominent politicians, notably Giolitti, Salandra, Facta and Orlando, and these leaders actively disliked one another. In such circumstances it was not surprising that the three Italian governments between May 1921 and October 1922 were fragile and unable to introduce the decisive measures needed to cope with the industrial disruption and the collapse of law and order.

This progressive collapse of law and order owed a great deal to

Fascist actions. *Squadrismo* continued through 1921. Socialists were attacked, and not infrequently killed. Fascist violence even extended to parliament itself, most notoriously on the occasion when a Socialist deputy was beaten up on the floor of the chamber.

  * Mussolini's activities during the remainder of 1921 were directed towards making Fascism a cohesive political force which could command more widespread support within Italian society. His attempt to organise Fascism more effectively resulted in the establishment of the *Partito Nazionale Fascista* in October 1921. Fascism was no longer a movement: it was now a political party. In the following month the party congress formally accepted Mussolini as the leader of Fascism. The party was to be organised and run by men from Mussolini's own Milan faction, who were loyal to their leader. Mussolini had established more control over those Fascist squads which had so terrorised Socialists in the agricultural areas of Emilia and the Romagna. However, his control over this provincial Fascism was by no means total, and there would be disagreements over the means to secure power. Yet he could now pose as the unchallenged head of a real political party.

  * Mussolini now increased his efforts to appeal to conservatives – people who feared Socialism, deplored the government's conciliatory policy towards labour, and questioned its ability to restore order. In November 1921 he made a direct attempt to appease catholics: Fascism was apparently opposed to divorce, in agreement with the *Popolari* that the peasants deserved a better deal, and prepared to settle the Roman question on terms acceptable to the Pope. Nothing more was heard of the the left-wing policies espoused by Fascism in 1919. In fact, the leader of Fascism had begun to distance himself from such radical ideas during 1920, and it had not been coincidental that the 35 Fascist deputies elected in May 1921 were on the right of the movement. From 1921 Mussolini's speeches concentrated on what Fascism was against, namely Socialism and Liberalism, but spelled out Fascist policies only in very broad terms, stressing its patriotism and commitment to strong government. A good example of this approach is the speech he gave in September 1922 in the city of Udine.

1 Our programme is simple: we wish to govern Italy. They ask us
   for programmes, but there are already too many. It is not
   programmes that are wanting for the salvation of Italy, but men
   and will-power.
5   . . . our political class is deficient. The crisis of the Liberal
   State has proved it . . . We must have a State which will simply
   say: 'The State does not represent a party, it represents the nation
   as a whole, it includes all, is over all, protects all.'
       This is the State which must arise from the Italy of Vittorio
10 Veneto. A State which does not acknowledge that the strongest
   power is right; which is not like the Liberal State, which, after

fifty years of life, was unable to install a temporary printing press so as to issue its paper when there was a general strike of printers; a State which does not fall under the power of the Socialists . . .
15 we want to remove from the State all its economic attributes. We have had enough of the State railwayman, the State postman and the State insurance official. We have had enough of the State administration at the expense of Italian tax-payers, which has done nothing but aggravate the exhausted financial condition of
20 the country. It still controls the police, who protect honest men from the attacks of thieves . . . [and] the army which must guarantee the inviolability of the country and foreign policy.

Such speeches were cynical attempts to persuade the conservative classes that they had not nothing to fear and much to gain from the victory of Fascism. They also reflected Fascism's lack of specific, detailed policies. Mussolini wanted a strong, expansionist Italy, hated Socialism and democracy, and despised parliament, but he was principally concerned with winning power for himself and becoming dictator of Italy. Policy was completely subordinated to this end. In fact, it was advantageous to have little clear policy – no groups would be offended.

Mussolini's approach produced results. By the end of 1921 the Fascist Party had 200,000 members. It was attracting not only ex-servicemen and radical students but also landowners, shopkeepers, and clerical workers. Many people who had previously supported the conservative wing of Liberalism now despaired of the seemingly ineffectual parliamentary system and saw Fascism as a way of securing the disciplined state for which they longed. However, it would be wrong to conclude that Fascism was hi-jacked by conservatives. The Fascist leaders in the provinces still thought of themselves as leading a revolutionary movement that would overthrow the state by force in a *coup d'etat*. Men like Roberto Farinacci, Italo Balbo, and Dino Grandi remained dedicated to violent *squadrismo*.

Mussolini was concerned that the increasing Fascist violence, even if directed at Socialists, might go too far and provoke conservatives to demand that the authorities crush the Fascists and restore law and order. This was a real danger and it was clear to Mussolini that the police and army had the power to destroy his movement. That he managed to calm conservatives, yet avoid splits within his party was proof of his political skills. On the one hand he encouraged the squads to continue their campaign of violence and suggested that he agreed with their plans for a violent seizure of power. On the other hand, when talking to conservatives, he disassociated himself from the worst excesses of Fascist violence. He would suggest that the perpetrators were renegades whom he would discipline, but would also imply that only he could curb these excesses. If conservatives wanted to avoid a violent conflict with Fascism they should deal with him. If they conceded some share of political power to Fascism, he would ensure that Fascism became a more respectable party.

This dual policy was followed throughout 1922. In the spring Fascist squads rampaged through north-central Italy attacking Socialist town councils and trade union property. In May the town council of Bologna was actually driven out of office. During July street-fighting took place in most of the northern cities. During this time Mussolini talked to the various Liberal factions, stressing Fascist power but also suggesting that he was far from being a rabid revolutionary. He implied that he was interested in a parliamentary alliance that would bring the Fascists into government. In such circumstances the fragile government coalition lacked the political will to use the police to curb the violence of a party which might soon be joining them in office. In any case, the police were reluctant to intervene in the street-fighting – they had no love for the Socialists and in some areas they had even loaned weapons to the local Fascist squads.

* At the end of July the socialist trade unions called a general strike in an attempt to force the government to act against the Fascists. Mussolini made brilliant use of this opportunity to demonstrate that the left was still a threat and that only Fascism could deal with it. As soon as the general strike was announced, he publicly declared that if the government did not stop the industrial action his Fascists would step in and do it for them. Almost immediately the strike began, Fascists took over the running of public transport and ensured that the postal system continued to function. If strikers protested they were beaten up. The general strike proved a fiasco for the Left. It had been poorly organised, and only attracted partial support from the workers. Even in those cities where the strike call was obeyed, the Fascist action limited its effect. Within days the strike had collapsed, leaving the Socialists in disarray. Mussolini could present his Fascists as the sole defenders of law and order. This was a crucial development. The Fascists' actions impressed the conservative middle classes, helping to convince them that Fascism could be trusted with a share in government. From this point on the question was not whether the Fascists would enter the government, but rather on what terms.

8 The March on Rome

Mussolini launched himself into further negotiations with the Liberal factions, discussing which cabinet posts should be allocated to the Fascists. He did not disclose that his real ambition was to be prime minister. At the same time he was talking to the Fascist squads about organising a *coup d'etat*. In fact, he was under great pressure to adopt such a policy – many Fascists had wanted to try to seize power at the end of the abortive general strike and it had taken all of Mussolini's authority to dissuade them. He believed that he could achieve power without a coup, but by considering such action he could keep his more radical supporters happy and intimidate the liberals into making concessions. At the beginning of October Mussolini increased the pressure by starting to organise a Fascist march on Rome.

The Fascist squads were organised into a militia and plans were drawn up to seize the major towns and cities of northern and central Italy. Around 30,000 Fascists would then converge on the capital and install themselves in power. If they met resistance they would crush it. Many Fascists genuinely believed that their coup was finally at hand. However, their leader saw the march as his ultimate piece of political blackmail. Mussolini seems to have been convinced that, under such a threat, the politicians would agree that he should become prime minister.

While going ahead with preparations for the march Mussolini took care to reassure the establishment that they need not fear a Fascist government. In particular, he stressed that Fascism and the monarchy could work together, as the following speech, which he made at Naples on the eve of the march, makes clear.

1 There is no doubt that the unity of Italy is soundly based on the House of Savoy. There is equally no doubt that the Italian monarchy, both by reason of its origin, development and history, cannot put itself in opposition to the new national forces. It did
5 not manifest any opposition when the Italian people – who, even if they were a minority, were a determined and intelligent minority – asked and obtained their country's participation in the war. Would it then have reason to be in opposition today, when *Fascismo* does not intend to attack the regime, but rather to free it
10 from all those superstructures that overshadow its historical position and limit the expansion of the national spirit?

The parliament and all the paraphernalia of democracy have nothing in common with the monarchy. Not only this, but neither do we want to take away the people's toy – the parliament.
15 We say 'toy' because a great part of the people seem to see it this way. Can you tell me else why, out of 11 million voters, 6 million do not trouble themselves to vote? But we will not take it away.

Mussolini realised that the attitude of the king was critical. As commander-in-chief he could order the army to crush Fascism if he so wished.

* By the last week of October preparations were complete. On the night of the 27th, Fascist squads seized town halls, telephone exchanges and railway stations throughout northern Italy. In the early hours of 28 October the government of Luigi Facta finally found the courage to act, and persuaded the king to agree to the declaration of a state of siege.

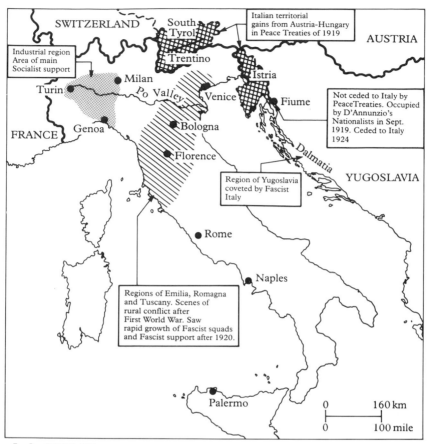

Italy 1918-25

Police and troops prepared to disperse the Fascist columns converging on Rome by road and rail. However, by 9am King Victor Emmanuel had changed his mind . He now refused to authorise the declaration of martial law which would have sanctioned the use of force against the Fascists. This would prove to be a fateful decision: it was a sign that the king lacked confidence in his government and was anxious to avoid a violent showdown with Mussolini's Fascists. It is still uncertain why Victor Emmanuel made this decision – he may have over-estimated the number of Fascists marching on Rome and feared a civil war; he may have feared that his cousin, the Duke of Aosta, a known Fascist sympathiser was waiting to depose him if he acted against Mussolini. Probably more plausibly, the king had little love for the existing Liberal politicians and, believing Mussolini's protestations of loyalty, considered that Fascists should be brought into the governing coalition.

Their nationalism, their anti-socialism and their energy might breath new life into the regime. Victor Emmanuel certainly did not realise that his decision would open the way for a Fascist dictatorship.

On hearing of the king's refusal to declare martial law, Facta's government resigned. Victor Emmanuel then approached Salandra, a veteran conservative-Liberal, and asked him to form a new government. Salandra attempted to negotiate with the Fascists, offering them a few cabinet posts, but it soon became apparent that Mussolini would accept nothing less than the post of prime minister for himself. With other Liberal leaders also opposed to a Salandra premiership – a sign of the continuing faction-fighting – the king realised that he needed to find a different man to head the government. In the apparent absence of any other viable candidate Benito Mussolini was asked, on 29 October, to become the prime minister of Italy.

Making notes on 'The Rise of Fascism'

Your notes on this chapter should include a brief biography of Mussolini himself, but should concentrate on identifying those factors which weakened the Liberal regime and enabled Fascism to grow and eventually take power. The following headings, sub-headings and questions should help you.

1.   Italy at war – Caporetto and Vittorio Veneto.
2.   The human and financial cost of the First World War – inflation; the effect of the end of the war on industry.
2.1 Labour militancy and unemployment.
3.   The 'socialist threat' – why were the middle classes and conservatives so fearful?
4.   Mutilated Victory – why was the government blamed?
4.1 Occupation of Fiume.
5.   Mussolini and the birth of Fascism – early life and political beliefs.
5.1 Mussolini and the First World War.
5.2 Establishment of the Fascist movement.
6.   Rise of Fascism 1919–21 – problems caused by the 1919 election.
6.1 *Popolari* – attitude to Liberalism and internal divisions.
6.2 Giolitti's government – socialist challenges in the factories and in the countryside.
6.3 Conservative backlash – rise of *Squadrismo*; who joined the squads?
6.4 1921 Electoral alliance.
7.   Mussolini seizes the initiative May 1921–October 1922 – what was his strategy? Why were governments unstable?
7.1 Forging Fascism into a cohesive force – PNF formed; what did Fascism stand for and who did it appeal to?

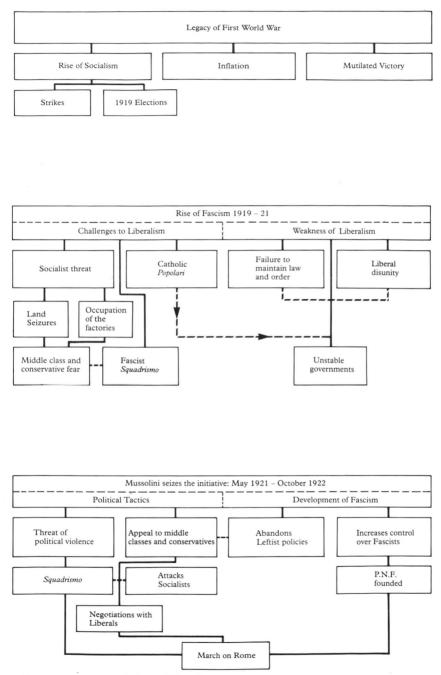

Summary – The Rise of Fascism

7.2 Mussolini's dual policy – violence and moderation.
7.3 General Strike of July 1922 – significance?
8.   March on Rome – what was its purpose?
8.1 Mussolini becomes prime minister. Why did the king appoint him?

Source-based questions on 'The Rise of Fascism'

1 The Fascist Programme and Mussolini's speeches

1 Carefully read the four extracts – the Fascist Programme of 1919, on page 48, and Mussolini's speeches on pages 51, 53, 54, and 56. Answer the following questions.

- a) Which aspects of the 1919 programme would be particularly offensive to conservatives? Why? (*3 marks*)
- b) Explain the meaning of the following extract from Mussolini's Bologna speech, (page 51 line 14), 'it is sad, after having fought the external enemy, to have to fight the enemy within'. (*3 marks*)
- c) What grounds did Mussolini have for declaring that the 'Socialists had formed a State within a State' (page 51 line 15)? (*4 marks*)
- d) Summarise Mussolini's attitude to Fascist violence, in your own words. Why might Mussolini have chosen this occasion, Bologna April 1921, to make such remarks? (*6 marks*)
- e) How did Fascist policy, as revealed by the 1919 programme and Mussolini's speech at Udine in 1922 (page 53), change over this three-year period? Why did Mussolini abandon the 1919 programme? (*6 marks*)
- f) What criticism does Mussolini level at Liberalism in his Udine speech? (*4 marks*)
- g) What was the purpose of Mussolini's speech at Naples in October 1922 (page 56)? (*4 marks*)

CHAPTER 4

Mussolini: From Prime Minister to Dictator 1922–6

1 Consolidating Power

On 30 October 1922 Mussolini arrived in Rome to be formally appointed prime minister of Italy. His Fascist blackshirts were now permitted to enter the city and they paraded in triumph before their leader.

Mussolini held the top political post in the land, but his dream of complete, unchallenged personal power was still a long way from realisation. Although many of his blackshirts believed that the Fascist revolution was about to begin, their leader showed caution. He had a more realistic appreciation of the limits of Fascist power. Mussolini was aware that a wholly Fascist government was not yet possible – such a government could not command a majority in parliament and the king, no doubt supported by the army, would probably not allow him to dispense with parliament. The new prime minister would have to construct a coalition government.

Mussolini's first administration contained 14 senior ministers of whom only four were Fascists, the majority being Liberals and *Popolari*. This reassured those conservatives and Liberals who saw Fascism simply as a useful tool with which to crush the Left. They had supported the Fascist entry into government on these grounds and believed that once the Socialists had been destroyed they could either absorb Fascism into the regime or dispense with it altogether. After all, Fascism lacked a coherent ideology and a clear set of policies, and was, therefore, unlikely to last for long.

* However, Mussolini was determined to be no-one's pawn. Fascists might be a minority in the governing coalition but he held not only the post of prime minister but also the powerful positions of minister of the interior and minister of foreign affairs. Above all, Mussolini was determined not to lose the momentum built up by the 'March on Rome'. He might not yet be able to secure supreme power but he would continue to use the threat of Fascist violence to intimidate parliament. At the same time he would attempt to persuade deputies that if they granted him near-dictatorial powers, they would be acting both in their own interests and in the interests of Italy itself. He would seek to convince them that the breakdown of law and order was so serious and the threat of Bolshevik revolution so great that extraordinary measures were needed to deal with the situation. His argument would be that, once the condition of the country had been stabilised, he would surrender his special powers and revert to normal parliamentary rule.

Of course, the Socialist threat was nearly non-existent and the collapse of law and order was largely the result of Fascist violence, but conservatives and Liberals remained mesmerised by the supposed danger from the Left. They also genuinely believed Mussolini's assurances that any new powers they granted him would be surrendered at the earliest suitable opportunity. Most would remain convinced until at least late 1924 that Mussolini could be 'transformed' into a respectable, even traditional, prime minister and that his movement could be found a place within the regime. This was to prove a fatal miscalculation. By the time these politicians realised their error it was already too late – the dictatorship was largely in place, parliament was increasingly an irrelevance, and open opposition was extremely hazardous.

The new prime minister took immediate action to increase his power, demanding that parliament grant him the right to rule by decree for 12 months. This would mean that the government could effectively create new laws without consulting parliament. Mussolini justified this demand by stating that only a strong, unfettered government could take the stern measures that were necessary to restore law and order and to put the country back on its feet. In attempting to convince parliament to give him these extraordinary powers, he delivered a speech which was carefully designed to stress the military strength of Fascism, but at the same time to reassure the deputies that he was not about to overthrow the state or to introduce a set of radical policies.

 1 I am here to defend and give the greatest value to the revolution of
   the 'blackshirts', inserting it intrinsically in the history of the
   nation as an active force in development, progress and the
   restoration of equilibrium. I could have carried our victory much
 5 further, and I refused to do so. I imposed limits upon my action
   . . . With three hundred thousand young men, fully armed, ready
   for anything and almost religiously prompt to obey any command
   of mine, I could have punished all those who have slandered the
   Fascisti and thrown mud at them. I could have made a bivouac of
10 this gloomy hall; I could have shut up Parliament and formed a
   government of Fascisti exclusively; I could have done so, but I
   did not wish to do so, at any rate at the moment.
       I have formed a coalition government, not with the intention of
   obtaining a Parliamentary majority, with which at the moment I
15 can perfectly well dispense, but in order to gather in support of
   the suffering nation all those who, over and above questions of
   party and section, wish to save her.
       From the bottom of my heart I thank all those who have
   worked with me, both Ministers and Under-Secretaries. I believe
20 also that I shall be giving expression to the thoughts of a large part
   of this assembly, and certainly of the majority of the Italian
   people, if I pay a warm tribute to our Sovereign, who, by refusing

to permit the useless reactionary attempts made at the eleventh
hour to proclaim martial law, has avoided civil war and allowed
25 the fresh and ardent Fascisti to pour itself into the sluggish
mainstream of the State.

Before arriving here we were asked on all sides for a programme. It is not, alas, Programmes that are wanting in Italy, but men
to carry them out. All the problems of Italian life have long since
30 been solved on paper; but the will to put these solutions into
practice has been lacking. The government today represents that
firm and decisive will.

The chamber gave him a massive vote of confidence and granted him
emergency powers for the 12 month period. Only the Socialists and
Communists opposed the motion – prominent Liberals including
Giolitti, Salandra and Facta proclaimed their support for this decisive
new prime minister.

* Mussolini now moved to consolidate his position. In December he
tried to increased his authority over his own party by establishing the
Grand Council of Fascism. This would be the supreme body within the
movement, discussing proposals to be put before the government. By
claiming the right to make all appointments to the Grand Council, he
was attempting to ensure that he alone controlled Fascist policy. In the
following month he reduced the influence of provincial Fascist leaders
still further by converting the Fascist squads into a national militia paid
for by the state. He now possessed a private army of over 30,000 men,
which he continued to use to intimidate potential opponents.

* Mussolini encouraged Fascist violence to deter potential opponents
but he also actively wooed influential groups. By early 1923 he had
persuaded the employers' organisation, *Confindustria*, to support his
premiership. The government's decision to drop Giolitti's proposal to
launch an attack on widespread tax evasion no doubt helped to convince
industrialists that the new prime minister was no dangerous radical.

Mussolini even managed to secure the tacit support of the Church by
confirming that he intended to ban contraception and to make religious
education compulsory in state schools. In response, the Pope began to
withdraw Vatican support from the *Popolari*, to the point of expelling
its leader, the priest Don Sturzo, from Italy. By mid 1923 the *Popolari*
had been dropped from the governing coalition and had lost the
backing of conservative catholics. Its political significance was now
effectively at an end.

2 Electoral Reform

Confident of the solid support of conservatives, many catholics and the
majority of Liberals, Mussolini introduced a bill to reform the electoral
system. This proposed that the political party securing the most votes

in a general election, provided it polled one quarter of the votes cast, should be allocated two-thirds of the seats in the chamber of deputies. This was a revolutionary idea. Mussolini defended it by stating that such a reform would produce governments with secure majorities and would thus enable them to deal decisively with Italy's problems. It would put an end to weak coalition governments which were terrified to act in case some of their supporters deserted them. These coalitions, so Mussolini claimed, had plagued Liberal Italy and helped to bring the country to its knees. Of course, the prime minister neglected to point out that if the bill became law it would become virtually impossible to vote the Fascists out of power. Given the command, the Fascist squads would smash up the presses of hostile newspapers and would physically prevent opposition voters from reaching the polling booths. As Mussolini was minister of the interior, he could instruct the police to stand aside as Fascists wreaked havoc. The potential to fix elections was enhanced by the fact that the minister had promoted Fascist sympathisers to important positions in local government.

When the bill was debated in parliament in July 1923 it secured an overwhelming majority. The fact that armed blackshirts had roamed the chamber during the debate undoubtedly intimidated deputies, but the support for Mussolini's proposal was not simply the result of fear. Many deputies genuinely approved of the repressive actions taken by the government against what they still viewed as the dangerous, revolutionary Left. Arrests and beatings were what these people needed! Other deputies welcomed the end of those seemingly impotent coalition governments which Italy had seen since the end of the war. However, the most important factor was the continuing belief that Mussolini and his Fascists were not enemies of parliamentary government and that 'normality' would be restored as soon as circumstances permitted. Mussolini had assured the chamber on more than one occasion that he had no desire to dispense with parliament. The fact that he was the head of a coalition government and was prepared to discuss the possibility of an electoral alliance with conservative groups seemed proof of his good faith. Giolitti and Salandra pledged their support for the bill and were joined by the great majority of Liberals.

The new electoral reform, known as the Acerbo Law, was put into practice in April 1924. In the general election of that month the Fascists, joined in an electoral pact by right-wing Liberals including Salandra, secured 66 per cent of the vote. Fascist deputies increased from 35 to 374, giving the party a clear majority in the 535 seat chamber. Mussolini had certainly grown in public popularity, but widespread blackshirt violence and Fascist ballot-rigging had contributed significantly to the party's vote. In fact, despite the intimidation, the opposition parties – principally the Socialists and Communists – had still managed to attract 2.5 million votes.

3 The Murder of Matteotti

When parliament reopened opposition deputies tried to publicise illegal Fascist actions at the polls. Their most prominent spokesman, the Socialist Giacomo Matteotti, produced evidence detailing Fascist violence and terror during the election campaign. On 10 June 1924, within days of these allegations being made, Fascist thugs abducted Matteotti in broad daylight and stabbed him to death. This brutal murder shocked not only Mussolini's political enemies but also many Liberals who thought the Fascists had finally gone too far. Mussolini denied all knowledge of the crime but, when evidence purporting to link the prime minister to the murder began to appear in the press, public opinion seemed to turn against him. At this point, opposition deputies walked out of parliament and set up their own assembly. These deputies, mainly Socialist, Communist and dissident *Popolari*, hoped that their 'Aventine secession' (named after a similar event in ancient Rome) might encourage the king to dismiss Mussolini. The Fascist leader's position appeared vulnerable.

* However, the king refused to contemplate the dismissal of Mussolini, fearing that such a decision would only strengthen the revolutionary Left and might lead to civil war. He was encouraged in this belief by leading Liberals and conservatives who saw the affair not as an opportunity to dispose of the Fascist leader but rather as a chance to increase their influence over the weakened prime minister. Giolitti and Salandra, for example, still supported Mussolini's premiership. For such men there appeared at that moment to be no viable or palatable alternative to the Fascist leader.

4 Emergence of the Dictatorship

While his position was being supported by these conservative interests, Mussolini moved to forestall any further opposition. In July 1924 he introduced press censorship and in the following month banned meetings by opposition political parties. But, despite the government's efforts, the controversy raised by the Matteotti affair did not disappear. Those Liberal leaders who had previously supported the government joined the opposition in November in protest against press censorship. Eventually, in December 1924, leading Fascists, exasperated by the uncertainty created by the affair and frustrated by the government's lack of radicalism, presented Mussolini with an ultimatum. If he did not end the Matteotti affair immediately and move decisively towards the establishment of a dictatorship, they would withdraw their support. The prime minister bowed to their demands and, in a speech on 3 January 1925, told parliament that he accepted responsibility for all Fascist actions up to that date:

1 I declare before all Italy that I assume full responsibility for what
   has happened . . . If fascism has turned out to be only castor oil
   and rubber truncheons instead of being a superb passion inspiring
   the best youth of Italy, I am responsible . . . Italians want peace
5 and quiet, and to get on with its work. I shall give it all these, if
   possible in love, but if necessary by force.

He was signalling that he would now take the measures necessary to
give himself more complete personal power. Even now his speech was
cheered in the chamber. With a clear majority in parliament and
confident that the king would not move against him, Mussolini created
his dictatorship. What opposition there was in the chamber proved no
threat – it was divided, lacking in leadership and compromised by its
earlier support for Fascism.

In January 1925 the prime minister established a committee to
reform the constitution. In December the *Legge Fascistissime* was
passed banning opposition political parties and free trade unions. Press
censorship was strengthened, a new secret police was set up, and a
special court was established to try political crimes. Fascist control of
local government was increased by replacing elected mayors with
nominated officials, known as *podestas*. In January 1926 Mussolini was
granted the right to issue decrees carrying the full force of law. He
could now circumvent parliament altogether. His personal rule was
enshrined in law.

Final touches to the dictatorship were added in 1928 when the king
lost the right to select the prime minister. In future a list of possible
candidates would be drawn up by the Grand Council of Fascism, a body
controlled by Mussolini, and the king would have to make his selection
from this list.

5 Reasons for Mussolini's Success

Was Mussolini's success the result of Liberalism's weakness or Fascism's strength?

The Fascist entry into government in October 1922 was not an armed
seizure of power: it was the result of a constitutional process. The king,
supported by the Liberal establishment, invited Mussolini to become
prime minister. They believed that he could be controlled as part of a
coalition government, and could be transformed into a respectable
politician. Events proved them wrong. October 1922 was clearly a
decisive moment in Italian history, signalling that the end of the Liberal
regime was imminent. That Liberal politicians could have invited the
very agent of their own destruction to take power was testament both to
the desperate straits in which the regime found itself after the First
World War, and to the skill of Mussolini in convincing the political
Establishment that he alone could help them to solve their problems.

There is still dispute among historians about the stability of the Liberal regime in the years before the war, but there is no doubt that it had failed to attract the active allegiance of many, if not most, Italians. The First World War was to bring to the fore the extent to which the regime was supported.

As industry expanded, Socialism found new converts and, inspired by the events of 1917 in Russia, the movement looked towards the revolutionary overthrow of the state. This, of course, terrified both the rich and the middle classes, particularly when the introduction of universal manhood suffrage enabled the Socialists to become the largest political party in parliament in 1919. The propertied classes looked to the government for reassurance but they were disappointed. Liberal governments preferred to remain neutral in industrial and agricultural disputes. There was to be no crackdown on strikers. The impression of government weakness was increased by the supposed failure to advance Italian interests at the peace conference. Italians of conservative disposition began to yearn for a more dynamic government which would restore law and order and protect their interests.

At this time of economic disruption and social ferment, the regime was losing credibility in the eyes of those very people it relied upon for support. In such circumstances many radical political groups emerged, of which Fascism was just one. Such groups did not enjoy mass support, but they did attract those who felt alienated from society, notably disillusioned ex-soldiers, and those who desired a dramatic, exciting style of politics. What distinguished the Fascists from the other small radical and nationalist groups was their leader.

Mussolini possessed a dynamic and dominant personality and proved himself a brilliant propagandist. For example, his *Popolo d'Italia* took every opportunity to exaggerate the socialist threat and to denounce Liberal incompetence and supposed cowardice. Fascists were depicted as selfless individuals devoted to creating their vision of Italy, an Italy of peace and stability, an Italy of social harmony, an Italy respected in the world. Fascists had the youth and the energy to embark on such a crusade. This image would prove attractive to many Italians.

Nevertheless, Mussolini was fortunate that the conflicts between landlords and Socialist peasants in central-northern Italy erupted into open violence at the end of 1920. This enabled his squads to become the vanguard of a conservative backlash. Although he had not created the situation, he was quick to take advantage of it. Realising that the route to power lay through cultivating conservatives, he abandoned the remnants of the radical programme set out in 1919. He encouraged Fascist violence in order to undermine law and order and thus erode the credibility of the government still further. At the same time he was careful to appear as essentially a moderate when talking to conservatives. He avoided committing himself to any clear policy programme and altered his message according to the audience he was addressing.

Mussolini would speak to Fascists of his determination to transform Italian society radically, yet tell conservatives that his real goal was simply to destroy Socialism and to inject some energy into the political system.

From small and inauspicious beginnings Mussolini had, by May 1921, persuaded the leading Liberal, Giolitti, to offer Fascism an electoral alliance. He built on this breakthrough into national politics and was determined not to surrender the initiative. As violence increased and the coalition governments appeared increasingly impotent, Fascism became a more credible political force. Mussolini's opportunism and keen tactical sense was displayed when the Socialists declared a general strike in the summer of 1922. By using his squads to attack strikers he emphasised his anti-Socialist credentials, and by calling off his men once the strike had collapsed he reassured conservatives that he could be trusted.

By October 1922 most Liberal leaders considered that there was no alternative to a Fascist entry into the coalition government. Moreover, they believed there was little to fear from such a development. They did not even realise, until the parliamentary crisis at the end of October, that Mussolini intended to be prime minister. The illusion that Fascism was no threat to the regime persisted at least until the murder of Matteotti in 1924, and by then it was too late. Although the king could have dismissed his prime minister in late 1924, it was not surprising that Victor Emmanuel declined to do so – he had no great love for the parliamentary regime, he feared Fascist strength, and he was well aware that the opposition to Mussolini was weak and divided.

That Liberals remained so convinced that Fascism could be transformed was largely the result of Mussolini's political skills, but it also points to a crisis of confidence within the regime itself. Liberals were afraid of the growing strength of Socialism and were unsure what a government could or should do in a time of economic dislocation and class tension. The advent of mass democracy meant that parliament was no longer the preserve of Liberals, yet the Liberal leaders tried to maintain the old style of politics. There was still no coherent Liberal party. There was just a series of factions based around prominent personalities. The Liberal governments of the post war years were, in consequence, particularly fragile coalitions unable and often unwilling either to grant reform or to direct the forces of the state (the police and the army) to uphold the law. Governments lost control of events and politics began to take to the streets.

A strong government of the centre-right might well have reassured conservatives and made the growth of Fascism more difficult, but such a government would have required the Liberal factions to join together and form a genuine parliamentary alliance with the *Popolari*. However, the Liberal tradition militated against such an arrangement with the party of organised catholicism. Furthermore, the *Popolari* fully reciprocated the Liberals' mistrust and were divided over the crucial issues of social and economic reform. Giolitti did try to form a working alliance with the *Popolari* in 1921 but mutual mistrust ensured that the coalition was short-lived. In such circumstances, it was not surprising that some Liberals began to see Fascism as a more acceptable coalition partner than the unreliable and disorganised catholics.

Finding themselves in a minority in parliament in 1919 and faced by hostile Socialists and distrustful *Popolari*, the Liberals were bound to be in difficulty. Severe economic problems, growing social tensions, and post-war disillusionment raised the political temperature still further and plunged the regime into crisis. Slow to adapt to the realities of mass democracy, and exaggerating the threat from the Left, many Liberals began to despair of the future of parliamentary government. It was tribute to Mussolini's political skills that he could take advantage of this despair which was felt not just by Liberals but also by most other Italians of a conservative disposition. By October 1922 he had convinced such men that only a Fascist presence in government could crush the Socialists, revitalise parliament as an institution, and restore confidence in the regime.

Making Notes on 'Mussolini: from Prime Minister to Dictator, 1922–6'

When making notes on this chapter you should not only write about the laws which created the dictatorship. You should also record your own conclusions about how Mussolini managed to persuade so many politicians to support such laws and about the reasons why the Fascists came to power. The following headings, sub-headings and questions should help you to do this:

1. Coalition government – what were Mussolini's aims? What did Liberals and conservatives expect from his government?
1.1 Emergency powers – how did he persuade parliament to grant him these powers?
1.2 Mussolini increases his control over the Fascist movement.
1.3 Gaining support from the Church and industrialists. How and why?
2. Electoral reform – why was it passed? Effects?
3. Murder of Matteotti – why did it create such opposition?
3.1 The king refuses to act against Mussolini – why?
4. Emergence of the dictatorship – how did he curb opposition? How did he secure greater control over parliament and local government?
5. Why was Mussolini successful in gaining power?

Answering essay questions on 'The Rise of Fascism' and 'Mussolini: from Prime Minister to Dictator, 1922–6'

Examination questions on the reasons for the growth and success of Fascism are very common. The information on which to base an answer is found not only in this chapter and in the chapter on *The Rise of Fascism*, but also in chapter 2, covering the Liberal Monarchy.

Many questions are apparently straightforward, asking what factors contributed to the growth and success of Fascism. Another common type of approach is to present one or two possible factors and ask the candidate to assess their significance in explaining Fascist success.

1 What factors promoted the growth of Fascism in Italy?

is an example of the first approach. Quite naturally, most examinees are confident of their ability to tackle what appears to be a rather 'obvious' question such as this, but regularly many spoil their chances of achieving a high mark by rushing into writing their essays without proper planning. As a result, many answers are either narrative accounts of events in 1918–22 or, more frequently, take the form of a list of reasons for Fascist success. It is important to avoid these pitfalls! If you think carefully about the wording of the question (the first stage in any essay-planning process) you will see that you are required to examine not only the years 1918–22, but also the period before the war and the emergence of the dictatorship after 1922.

In drawing up an essay plan you should first make a list of reasons for the growth of Fascism. There might be as many as 12 items in your list. Then you should attempt to group these into three, four, or five general categories. For example, you might have categories headed 'Weaknesses of the regime', 'Legacy of the First World War' and 'Mussolini's political skills' etc. You could include the governments' lack of popular support in the first category. Each category will be dealt with in a separate section of your essay. Having categorised your list of reasons, you should think out one or two phrases in each case to explain how your category heading helped bring about the growth of Fascism. These can then form the basis of the opening sentences to each paragraph. Once you have done this, re-read your essay plan and decide in what order to write the paragraphs. What criteria would you use to decide on the order?

A similar approach can be adopted for questions such as

2 'The Socialist threat and the belief that Italy had suffered a mutilated victory in the First World War enabled Fascism to grow and take power.' How far do you agree with this statement?

Again you should draw up a list of reasons for Fascism's growth and success and then categorise these reasons. Two of the categories should be the ones stated in the essay title. As with the first quesion, you

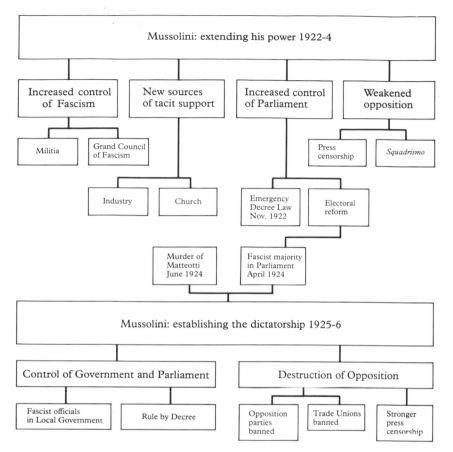

Summary – Mussolini: from Prime Minister to Dictator, 1922-6

should think of one or two phrases to explain how each category heading helped bring about Fascist success.

Now re-read what you have written, and attempt to distinguish those factors which were crucial to the rise of Fascism. Are the socialist threat and the mutilated victory critical factors? Your decision will determine the shape of your essay. If you conclude that they were the two most critical factors, you should state this clearly in your opening paragraph and devote the greater part of the essay to explaining why they were so important. However, if you decide that socialism and the mutilated victory were not the only crucial or the most crucial factors, you should state this in your opening paragraph and also say which were the (other) critical factors. Your next paragraphs should briefly describe the contribution of socialism and mutilated victory, but you should then go on to say why other factors were more or just as important.

Source-based questions on 'Mussolini: from Prime Minister to Dictator, 1922–6'

1 Prime Minister Mussolini and Parliament
Carefully read Mussolini's speech to parliament in November 1922 (page 62) and answer the following questions:
- a) Identify three phrases designed to reassure his listeners that he was not a revolutionary. (*3 marks*)
- b) Identify two passages designed to intimidate the deputies. (*3 marks*)
- c) What, according to Mussolini, is the policy of his government? Explain in your own words. (*5 marks*)
- d) How convincing is this statement of his policy? Explain your answer. (*6 marks*)
- e) How accurate were Mussolini's claims concerning the extent of his power in November 1922? Explain your answer. (*8 marks*)

CHAPTER 5

Mussolini and the Fascist Political System

1 Mussolini's Aim: Personal Dictatorship

By 1926 Mussolini had achieved his ambition of making himself the dictator of Italy. He could make laws simply by issuing decrees. Parliament was under his full control – no longer a forum for debate, but simply a theatre in which his decisions could be applauded by Fascist supporters and sympathisers. With Liberals and *Popolari* divided and leaderless, and the Socialists under constant physical attack, organised political opposition did not exist. Of course, technically Mussolini could still be dismissed by the king, but the 'March on Rome' and the 'Matteotti Affair' had proved that Victor Emmanuel was not prepared to stand up to his prime minister. Furthermore, providing the king remained in fear and awe of the Fascist leader, Mussolini need not worry about the armed forces, as they were very unlikely to break their pledge of loyalty to the monarch.

With his position secure, Mussolini now set out to create his Fascist state. This state was to be a personal dictatorship, for the prime minister's central goal was to maintain and increase his own personal power. In pursuit of this aim he encouraged a cult of personality which stressed his genius, his power and his indispensability as leader of the nation. He attempted to consolidate his position by seeking a constructive working relationship with powerful interest groups, notably the Church, the industrialists, and the armed forces.

His pursuit of personal power took precedence over the desire to 'Fascistise' Italy and Italian institutions. This policy disappointed many in the Fascist party who hoped that the Fascist revolution would sweep away interest groups and create a state in which the party controlled all the organs of government. Their leader still talked of revolution, but he was determined that the party should be his servant and not he its agent. Mussolini would decide what powers the party should possess, what Fascist policy should be and how and when it should be implemented.

The Italy Mussolini created was one in which he alone possessed ultimate power. Interest groups, the old institutions of government and the Fascist party all competed against each other for authority, but they looked to Mussolini to adjudicate their disputes and to make the final decisions. Without him government could not function and the regime would collapse.

2 The Cult of Personality

The cult of Mussolini, or of '*il Duce*', as he was increasingly to be known, had begun by 1926. It was intended to build popular support for the dictator and to overawe potential opponents by stressing his supposed near super-human talents. He was to be portrayed not as just another politician but as Italy's saviour, a man chosen by destiny to save the country from the Socialist menace and corrupt democratic politicians and to restore Italian greatness. He was the new Caesar – a man of genius, a man of action, a man of culture, a statesman of world renown dedicated only to the revival of Italy.

Mussolini revives the ancient glories of Rome. He is viewing a statue of Julius Caesar which has been installed in the recently excavated Forum.

The regime used all the methods of propaganda at its disposal to convey its message. Government controlled newspapers stressed his benevolence and took particular pride in quoting the opinions of foreign admirers, particularly if they were leading statesmen. The British Foreign Secretary, Austen Chamberlain, was thus widely reported as saying that Mussolini was 'a wonderful man working for the greatness of his country', while Winston Churchill's opinion in 1927 that the Duce's 'sole thought was the lasting well-being of the Italian people as he sees it' received similar publicity. Mussolini's supposed dedication to duty led to stories that Mussolini toiled for up to 20 hours per day on government business. In fact, the light was left on in his study for most of the night to back up this claim and to disguise the fact that the dictator usually retired to bed rather early.

The newspapers also suggested that the Duce was infallible. 'Mussolini is always right' became a popular phrase, an idea the dictator encouraged with such utterances as 'often I would like to be wrong, but so far it has never happened and events have always turned out just as I foresaw'. To maintain this impression, Mussolini was quick to claim the credit for any successes and still quicker to blame others for any mistakes.

The Duce was keen to be portrayed as a vigorous, athletic and

Mussolini playing the violin.

courageous man – a model for all Italian males. Magazines and newspapers printed pictures of him horse-riding, enjoying winter sports, driving cars at high speed and flying airplanes. An image of youthfulness was maintained by the suppression of any references to his age or to the fact that he needed to wear glasses.

Not content with this, the dictator insisted that he must also be seen as a man of culture. Consequently it was made known that he had read and digested all 35 volumes of the Italian Encyclopaedia and had read nearly all the classics of European literature, including the complete works of William Shakespeare.

* His expectation that anyone might be taken in by this image and these exaggerated claims revealed Mussolini's own vanity and also his low opinion of the public. Indeed, he declared that the public 'are stupid, dirty, do not work hard enough and are content with their little cinema shows'. Mussolini believed that the masses were not really interested in debate or discussion but preferred to be told what to do. They would enjoy the belief that they were ruled by a near super-man and would feel proud that Italy was apparently so admired by the rest of the world. Spectacles, parades and constant propaganda would keep their interest and secure their allegiance. As Mussolini put it, 'one must always know how to strike the imagination of the public: that is the real secret of how to govern'.

Mussolini cutting the first sod of the new city of Aprilla on the former Pontine Marshes.

Mussolini encouraging the harvesters at Aprilla.

It is uncertain how many people were taken in by the 'Cult of Ducismo'. Many, perhaps most, must have been extremely sceptical, but it did make large numbers of Italians believe that there was no conceivable alternative to the Fascist regime. The sheer volume of propaganda stressing Mussolini's power and genius deterred potential opposition. To this extent the cult of personality certainly achieved its aim.

3 Mussolini and Government

Mussolini was determined to ensure that all real power rested in his hands – he alone would devise policy and he alone would make all major decisions. The king would be an irrelevance and cabinet, parliament, and the institutions of state would be his loyal servants.

King Victor Emmanuel was easily dealt with. The monarchy had traditionally distanced itself from domestic policy and concerned itself principally with foreign affairs. Mussolini realised that he completely over-awed Victor Emmanuel and took advantage of this to deter the monarchy from any political involvement. The dictator still followed protocol by visiting the king twice a week, but Victor Emmanuel was never asked his advice and was only told what Mussolini wanted him to hear.

Mussolini was not prepared to share power with his ministers. There would be no cabinet government whereby ministers helped work out policy for their own departments and freely discussed government strategy in cabinet meetings. There was to be no government 'team'. Instead, the role of ministers was simply to follow the Duce's instructions unquestioningly. In fact, Mussolini himself held the most important ministries – foreign affairs, interior and the three armed services – for the greater part of his time as dictator.

The Duce had even less regard for parliament. By 1926 it had lost its ability to discuss policy, to debate and amend proposed legislation, and to criticise the government. Its reputation and political significance was to sink still further in subsequent years. With opposition parties banned, the chamber was dominated by sycophantic Fascist deputies who did not even bother to vote formally on Mussolini's legislation: they simply shouted their assent. Elections as they had been known ceased to exist. The electorate was reduced to exclude most of the working classes who had previously supported the Socialists, all candidates had to be Fascist-approved, and the results were shamelessly rigged to show over 98 per cent approval for the regime. Eventually, in January 1939, parliament abolished itself altogether, to be replaced by the equally meaningless Chamber of Fasces and Corporations.

If cabinet and parliament were to be Mussolini's servants, then so too were the other institutions of the Italian state – the civil service, local government, the judiciary and the armed services. However, he was keen to achieve his goals without provoking the head on clash with these institutions that the radicals in the Fascist party desired. A wholesale sacking of personnel in the civil service, judiciary, and army officer corps and their replacement by Fascist party appointees would almost certainly have caused a crisis and would definitely have increased the power of the party. Mussolini wanted to avoid any such crisis and was anxious to restrict the power of the party and to keep it under his complete command. The dictator recognised that the conservatives, who were so prominent in the state institutions, were largely sympathetic towards him, if distrustful of the party radicals. He set out to capitalise on this sympathy by using his powers of patronage to reward loyalty and by introducing policies to which conservatives could give their support. However, at the same time, he made it clear that if his wishes were not supported and obeyed, he would be ruthless in seeking out and destroying opposition.

Mussolini's approach meant that there was no Fascist revolution in government. Indeed, the Fascist party complained that party membership was dangerously low in the institutions of state. In 1927, for instance, it was estimated that only some 15 per cent of the civil service was Fascist. Nevertheless, the civil service loyally carried out the instructions of its political master, the Duce. During the 1930s Fascist party membership did increase among civil servants, but this seems to have been largely the result of a recognition that promotion depended on being a card-carrying supporter of the regime.

The dictator adopted a similar policy in his dealings with the armed services. Mussolini emphasised that he and the military shared a common interest in expanding the armed forces and in pursuing an aggressive foreign policy. Further support was gained by promoting senior generals to the coveted post of Field Marshal. Ambitious officers soon came to realise that a pro-Fascist attitude, and preferably party membership, would enormously enhance their prospects of promotion. The army did, admittedly, resent the pretensions of the Fascist militia to be a significant military force but it was still willing to give its loyalty to the Duce.

Only with the judiciary did Mussolini conduct a purge of what he considered to be undesirable elements. Dozens of judges were sacked for being insufficiently sympathetic towards Fascism or for being too independent of the government. The dictator wanted to ensure that the judiciary could be relied upon to follow his government's instructions. The Italian legal system consequently lost all claim to impartiality. Imprisonment without trial became commonplace and, where cases did come to court, Mussolini occasionally intervened to dictate verdicts and sentences.

This determination to control all the institutions of the state also extended to local government. Local self-government was abolished and elected mayors and town councils were replaced by officials appointed from Rome.

Mussolini's methods ensured that he extended his power throughout the Italian state, building up support based on self-interest and avoiding unnecessary conflict. His tactics in pursuit of his goal of complete personal power varied between aggression and conciliation, according to the nature of the institution in question. He would adopt a similar variety of tactics when dealing with those interest groups whose support he needed to consolidate his regime – the Church, industry, and the Fascist party itself.

The Duce had wooed the Vatican even before he became prime minister, disavowing his earlier anti-clericalism and emphasising that the Church had nothing to fear from Fascism. In fact, a Fascist victory

would destroy the Pope's enemies – Socialism and Liberalism. Relations steadily warmed and in 1929 the Lateran Pacts were signed,
finally healing the breach between the Catholic Church and the Italian
state. Mussolini could now rely upon official catholic support for his
regime. The Duce's relations with the Church are analysed in detail on
pages 103–106.

Mussolini also adopted conciliatory tactics, at least to begin with,
when dealing with Italian industrialists. In the Vidoni Palace Pact of
1925 all socialist and catholic trade unions were banned and, in the
following year, strikes were outlawed. A fuller discussion of Fascism's
policy towards industry is to be found on page 98, but these early
concessions were instrumental in securing industrialists' loyalty to the
regime.

4 Mussolini and the Fascist Party

Once he was in power, Mussolini had to decide what should be the role
of his Fascist Party. Should the PNF quietly disband having helped its
leader gain political control of the country, or should it act as a radical
force transforming Italian society? Should it be a mass party or a
disciplined élite? The Duce seems to have found it difficult to decide on
these questions and his opinion varied over the years. However, his
mind was clear and his policy unchanging on what should be the
relationship between the leader and the party – the PNF would serve
the Duce and not vice versa.

From the time of the Fascist breakthrough into Italian politics in
1920–1, Mussolini had stressed the need for discipline and central
control. However, his struggle to assert his leadership had not been
easy. Local Fascist leaders, (ras), might acknowledge Mussolini as
Duce of Fascism, but they were reluctant to accept central direction. In
fact, their violent actions during 1921 and 1922 at times embarrassed a
leader who was trying to reassure conservatives that his movement
could be a dynamic yet responsible political force. The 'March on
Rome', which Mussolini used to brilliant effect as political blackmail,
was at least in part a concession to pressure from the radical *squadristi*.

Once he had been appointed prime minister, Mussolini moved to
extend his control over his party. The creation of the militia provided
paid employment for Fascist *squadristi* and helped to ensure their
continued loyalty. The establishment of the Grand Council of Fascism
as the supreme policy-making body for the movement strengthened the
leader's position still further since he appointed all its members. As he
rewarded loyalty, so he punished opposition – during 1923 local parties
were purged of active or potential dissidents. Despite these efforts,
Mussolini's control over the party was still not absolute, as the *ras*
demonstrated when, during the Matteotti crisis of 1924, they demanded that he establish a dictatorship.

If the *ras* and their *squadristi* hoped that the creation of a dictatorship would enhance party power, they were to be disappointed. Mussolini set up a personal dictatorship. With control over the institutions of state, his power was secure and he was no longer vulnerable to pressure from within the PNF. The Duce illustrated his mastery of the party at the last party congress, held in June 1925. Mussolini demanded that the party should end internal arguments and obey the orders of its leader. Dissenting voices were shouted down. Although it was scheduled to last three days, the convention lasted only a few hours. By the end of 1928 the Duce had organised a further purge of Fascists suspected of disloyalty and had established the principle that all party posts should be appointments made from party headquarters in Rome, a headquarters he, of course, controlled. The PNF had become totally subservient to its leader.

That Mussolini had managed to achieve absolute dominance over Fascism was testament to his political skills, but it also reflected the fact that without Mussolini there was nothing to hold the party together. The PNF was not a united, coherent movement but rather a broad, uneasy coalition of groups with differing political views. *Squadristi* demanded the continuance of violent raids, ex-socialists wanted the reorganisation of industry, nationalists desired the revision of the peace settlement, and conservatives hoped for the restoration of law and order and normality. Only Mussolini could provide unity. The disparate, disorganised factions came to recognise this and looked to win his interest and support. The dictator's concerns and enthusiasms would change over the years, and consequently he was sympathetic first to one faction then to another – first conciliatory to the conservatives to secure the support of interest groups such as industry, then enthusiastic for a reorganisation of industry into a corporate state, and in the late 1930s reverting to radical ideas of revolutionising Italian social habits. Of course, the real significance of this was that the Duce and not the party would be responsible for determining the course of Fascist policy.

* Given the party's subservience to its Duce, it was not surprising that the men who occupied senior posts within the party were notable less for their ability than for their obedience and powers of flattery. The most senior post, that of party secretary, was held by a succession of utterly loyal Fascists of very modest ability. Under such men as Achille Starace, party secretary from 1931–9, the PNF opened its doors to all those who saw party membership simply as a way to secure a safe job in the Fascist administration. By the mid-1930s workers and peasants, who had once made up almost 30 per cent of party membership, had become a tiny minority. The PNF now consisted overwhelmingly of white collar public employees.

Mussolini's promotion of second-rate officials showed his susceptibility to flattery, but it also revealed his continuing concern to prevent the emergence of potential rivals. Men of drive and apparent ability would find themselves moved far from the centre of power. For example, the young squad leader, Italo Balbo, who achieved fame in 1931 when he completed a trans-Atlantic flight, was soon sent to occupy a post of luxurious idleness in Libya. Another young *squadristi*, Dino Grandi, apparently had some ambition to succeed the Duce but found himself despatched to London as Italian ambassador, a post of honour but of little power. No serious rival to the Duce ever emerged. Indeed, even men who had made their name as radical *squadristi*, such as Roberto Farinacci, enthusiastically joined in the cult of the Duce. They realised that Mussolini was prepared to allow them to keep much of their power in the provinces providing they remained utterly loyal and obedient to him. They were also well aware that without Mussolini as dictator their own power would collapse.

5 Relations between Party and State

Although the party lost what dynamism it had once possessed and became a bloated bureaucracy offering secure, undemanding jobs to Fascist supporters, its continued existence gave it some importance in the government of Italy. In particular, the PNF represented a potential rival authority to that of the institutions of the state. Such rivalry was particularly common in the provinces where local party secretaries competed for power with provincial prefects. It was also seen to some extent in central government where departments of the civil service argued with the Fascist bureaucracy controlling the new Fascist corporations. In the armed forces there was rivalry between the Fascist militia and the regular army, the latter resenting the claim that blackshirt officers were equal in status to army officers. The army and militia also argued over the distribution of weapons between them.

In these rivalries and arguments over jurisdiction both sides would look to Mussolini to solve the disputes. This gave the Duce great power, since without his adjudication government could grind to a halt. At the same time, however, these disputes over which body had the power to take which decision made government slow and inefficient. With so many matters awaiting the Duce's personal decision, delays were unavoidable, despite his spurious claims to be working up to 20 hours each day. The dictator's determination that he should personally occupy the most important ministries of state only worsened the situation. When decisions were taken they were often made without proper thought or consultation, as when the Duce selected the air force's new fighter plane after only a most cursory glance at the relevant information. Mussolini's tenure of so many ministries also meant that he found it impossible to ensure that his decisions were actually being carried out as he had intended. Fascist government, then, was not nearly as streamlined and efficient as the Duce and his foreign admirers liked to suggest. Mussolini might have supreme personal power but below him there was all too often confusion, delay and incompetence.

6 Popular Support and Opposition

Mussolini's control over the Fascist party and the great institutions of state made open opposition both difficult and dangerous. As the death of Matteotti proved, the Duce had no compunction about using violence and even murder to silence his critics. The ban on political activity outside the Fascist party, together with the implementation of press censorship, denied opponents a platform for their views. Dissidents would be spied upon by the dictator's secret police, the OVRA, might be severely beaten up, and could be imprisoned without trial.

Faced with such an array of repressive measures, it was not surprising that opposition within Italy was disorganised and ineffective. Only two sizeable networks of anti-Fascists existed within the country. These were the communists and a group based around Carlo Roselli, who hoped to create an alliance between Socialists and Liberals opposed to the regime. Both organisations were forced to operate underground, doing little more than circulating literature and lifting their members' spirits. Neither group could claim more than 7,000 active supporters.

The lack of significant opposition within Italy was certainly a reflection of the strength of the regime's repressive machinery, but it was also proof that the dictator knew how to manipulate his subjects. Those Liberals and *Popolari* who had grown disillusioned with Fascism were usually left alone, providing they did not venture to criticise the regime openly. From time to time, a few individuals would be assaulted by the OVRA or the militia simply to remind others that conformity was the safest option.

Journalists and intellectuals who might have been expected vigorously to oppose a system which so enthusiastically suppressed individual freedoms were encouraged to join that system. Journalists had their pay doubled and were offered secure jobs in the profession. Given the easy rewards and the apparent impossibility of publishing critical material, most writers settled for the role of party hack or else avoided political journalism altogether. Mussolini offered similar inducements to academics and intellectuals. For example, Marconi, the inventor of radio, was created a marquis, while D'Annunzio of Fiume fame received a generous pension and a palatial villa for his services to Fascism. The Duce used his newly created Fascist Academy to offer plum jobs and fat salaries to leading professors. Few could resist such temptations, particularly when they were well aware that any sign of dissent would lead to their immediate dismissal.

The regime also used these tactics of fear and self-interest to deter opposition from the general public. Party membership became increasingly necessary for those seeking work or promotion in the public sector. Dissent could mean dismissal and persistent offenders might even be sent to some poor remote southern hill-town to serve a sentence of internal exile. However, the regime was determined not only to deter opposition but also to build up popular support. Extreme propaganda was its principal weapon. This propaganda, of which the Cult of the Duce was a very important part, stressed the genius of Mussolini, the impossibility of opposition, and the supposed achievements of Fascism. Much was heard of Fascist successes in foreign policy, such as Yugoslavia's cession of Fiume to Italy. Italians were informed that foreigners were loud in their admiration for the Duce and his policies. They were promised that Italy under Fascist rule would regain the greatness she had known under Ancient Rome and during the Renaissance. Mussolini hoped to capture the imagination of the public and to win their commitment to the transformation of Italians into a energetic, disciplined, obedient and warlike people. Parades, processions, the press, and education were all used in an attempt to convey the message that the present was one of the great moments in Italian history and that Italians had a duty to participate in this adventure.

It is uncertain how many Italians were fully convinced by this incessant propaganda – probably relatively few – but it appears that the Duce was personally very popular. For most Italians, at least until the late 1930s, the dictator was producing stability at home and success abroad. His regime seemed to be providing moderate prosperity without intruding too far into private lives and without making excessive demands on the public, while foreign adventures, as in Ethiopia, excited patriotic interest. Given this record, there seemed to be little need for opposition and, in any case, Italians were well aware that opposition was likely to prove highly dangerous.

It is significant that although the regime set up penal colonies on remote, inhospitable islands such as Lipari and Lampedusa, off the Italian mainland, these were on a much smaller scale than the Nazis' concentration camps for political dissidents. While several hundred thousand opponents of the Nazis were imprisoned Italian camps probably held fewer than 5,000 prisoners. Conditions were tough, and some torture did occur, but the brutality was not systematic. Mussolini might occasionally advocate vicious punishments for those who did actively oppose him but, in practice, Italian Fascism preferred to cajole its subjects into outward conformity, rather than ruthlessly to root out potential dissenters.

7 Comparison of Fascism and Nazism

The years between the First and Second World Wars have often been described as the era of the Fascist Dictators. The 1930s, in particular, have been seen as the heyday of European Fascism, with Italy,

Germany, and Spain all experiencing Fascist regimes. But what did these regimes (especially Fascism in Italy and Nazism in Germany) have in common? Did Italy provide a model for its German counterpart?

It is certainly true that both countries experienced the collapse of parliamentary democracy and its replacement by largely personal dictatorships. Economic problems, a weak party system, a perceived communist threat, and the existence of an Establishment uncommitted to the notion of mass democracy combined to cripple parliamentary government. In the resulting power vacuum it was possible for radical groups espousing anti-communist and anti-democratic opinions to grow. Mussolini and Hitler, as leaders of such groups, managed to convince their conservative Establishments that their parties posed no fundamental threat and deserved a chance to try to tackle the economic and political crises. Once in power, however, the leaders of Fascism and Nazism showed that they would neither share their power nor relinquish it.

* The parallel between the Italian and German dictators is striking. They shared an all-consuming desire for supreme personal power over their respective countries. They were determined that power should be theirs alone. They would not tolerate any control from the conservative Establishments that had helped them into power, nor were they prepared to be the servants of their own parties. The Fascist and Nazi parties would continue in existence, as would the great institutions of state, such as the civil service, but there could be no doubt where ultimate power lay.

They attempted to remove dissent and to build up support for their regimes by employing a judicious mixture of repression, concession, propaganda and foreign adventure. Censorship and legalised state violence curbed opposition. Working compromises were sought with powerful interest groups, notably the army and industry. A cult of personality was consciously promoted, stressing the leader's genius, vision, benevolence, and infallibility. Only the leader could restore national pride and secure the country's rightful place among the great European powers. This pre-eminent position was to be achieved, so the public was told, by a series of diplomatic coups or, if needs be, by war.

This approach was effective. Many ordinary people, particularly in Germany, were prepared to believe in the all-powerful, charismatic leader. The dictators' political style of dramatic, choreographed rallies, parades and spectacles suggested that here was an energetic alternative to dull and petty parliamentary politics. The American journalist William Shirer recorded his impressions of one of these rallies in Nazi Germany:

1 I'm beginning to comprehend, I think, some of the reasons for Hitler's astounding success . . . he is restoring pageantry and

colour and mysticism to the drab lives of twentieth century Germans.

5   The hall was a sea of brightly coloured flags. Even Hitler's arrival was made dramatic. The band stopped playing. There was a hush over 30,000 people packed in the hall. Then the band struck up the Badenweiler March, a very catchy tune and used only when Hitler makes his big entries. Hitler appeared at the
10   back of the auditorium and, followed by his aides, he strode slowly down the long centre aisle while 30,000 hands were raised in salute . . . In such an atmosphere no wonder, then, that every word dropped by Hitler seemed like an inspired word from on high. Man's – or at least the German's – critical faculty is swept
15   away at such moments and every lie pronounced is accepted as high truth itself.

Mussolini also recognised the importance of such a political style, as he explained in 1922:

Democracy has taken 'elegance' from the lives of the people, but Fascism brings it back; that is to say, it brings back colour, force, picturesqueness, the unexpected, mysticism, and in fact all that counts in the souls of the multitude.

These new leaders could speak powerfully to ordinary people – as one Italian writer explained.

1   Mussolini always knew how to speak a language that the people understood . . . He had all sorts of feelers and antennae that made him grasp the trend of the popular mood and suggested to him the right attitude, the right slogan, that could bring popular passion
5   to a frenzy.

Hitler possessed similar talents, as Otto Strasser, a one time political opponent within the Nazi party, attested.

1   Hitler responds to the vibration of the human heart with the delicacy of a seismograph . . . Adolf Hitler enters a hall. He sniffs the air. For a minute he gropes, feels his way, senses the atmosphere. Suddenly he bursts forth. His words go like an arrow
5   to their target.

Influenced by the personal dynamism of the leaders and grateful for the restoration of law and order and the return of apparent economic stability, it was possible to overlook the systematic attack on political freedoms and individual liberties. Believing, at least in part, the propaganda claim that the dictators were trying to create a better, less divided society, many citizens justified the state's intrusion into nearly every aspect of life. Work and leisure time, for both adults and young people, were increasingly controlled by the regime through such organisations as the Labour Front, Strength through Joy, and the Hitler Youth in Germany, and the *Dopolavoro* and ONB in Italy. Certainly, some people objected to this increase of control by the state, but most realised that conformity was the safest course and that the new organisations could provide some material benefits, notably subsidised leisure pursuits and holidays.

As the 1930s progressed, both Mussolini and Hitler became increasingly obsessed by dreams of foreign expansion – the Duce in the Mediterranean, Balkans and North Africa, and the Führer in Eastern Europe and Russia. To prepare their populations for the wars which they believed would be necessary to realise these expansionist aims, the dictators increased their attempts to militarise society. Through propaganda, education, youth training and re-armament, they tried to create a new kind of citizen – one who was obedient, disciplined, self-sacrificing and warlike. The dictators wanted to convince their publics that war was not something to be regretted, an admission of the failure of diplomacy, but rather was something to be welcomed. War was man's natural condition, and should be celebrated not decried. As Mussolini put it:

1 War alone brings up to their highest tension all human energies
  and puts the stamp of nobility upon the peoples who have the
  courage to meet it. Fascism carries this antipacifist struggle into
  the lives of individuals. It is education for combat. I do not
5 believe in perpetual peace; not only do I not believe in it but I find
  it depressing and a negation of all the fundamental virtues of man.

This stress on war and the attempt at the militarisation of society appealed to only a relatively small section of the population and must have irritated or appalled many ordinary Italians and Germans. However, as long as the dictators could continue to deliver foreign policy successes at minimum cost, their popularity was assured. Mussolini's own personal popularity reached a peak in the aftermath of the Ethiopian war, while Hitler's diplomatic victories over the Rhineland, Austria and the Sudetenland brought him massive support. To the citizens of Italy and Germany their leaders were finally restoring national pride and putting an end to the frustrations and humiliations caused by the peace treaties drawn up at the end of the First World War.

Those Germans and Italians who were impressed by the easy diplomatic victories of the 1930s were less enthusiastic about the prospect of a general European war. Berlin in 1939 and Rome in 1940 experienced none of the war hysteria that had been so widespread 25 years earlier on the outbreak of the First World War. Nevertheless, such was the faith in their leaders that the public remained confident that victory would be cheap and easy. Italians were soon relieved of this illusion, but most of their German counterparts, buoyed up by the defeat of France in 1940, were to keep their faith in the Führer until the very last months of the war.

The war, and the war alone, brought about the destruction of the two regimes, but not before the dictators had wreaked havoc on their own peoples and on Europe. Italy was fought over by foreign armies and fell into a bitter and bloody civil war. Germany saw millions of its citizens die and witnessed the destruction of its industry and infrastructure. The country itself was divided in two by the victorious powers.

If there were so many similarities between the Italian and German dictatorships is it possible to conclude that the Führer copied the Duce's methods? Hitler himself admitted that he had an admiration for the Duce and said that the 'March on Rome' in 1922 had provided a model for his own, abortive, 'Munich *Putsch*' one year later. Mussolini's use of propaganda and the promotion of a cult of personality provided Hitler with inspiration. Italian blackshirts and their violent, paramilitary methods influenced the Nazi SA, the brownshirts. Hitler may also have learned important lessons from Mussolini's courting of powerful conservative groups and the worried middle classes in the years immediately before and after 1922. The Italian regime's attempts to control its citizens' lives, via education, the ONB and the *Dopolavoro*, also provided some models for the Nazi state.

* However, despite these examples, it is possible to exaggerate the similarities between the dictatorships. The regimes were not carbon copies of one another. As Hitler himself remarked, 'from the failure of the Munich *putsch* I learnt the lesson that each country must evolve its own type and methods of national regeneration.' The differences between the two dictatorships were significant.

One notable difference between the regimes was in the degree of power the dictators could exercise over their citizens. The Nazi state compelled greater loyalty and obedience from its citizens. The regime's dramatic foreign policy successes brought Hitler a degree of popularity that the Duce could only envy. The Gestapo rooted out opposition more thoroughly than did its Italian equivalent, the OVRA. Even passive dissent was attacked. From the very beginning of the regime in 1933 the number of people finding themselves designated as political opponents or anti-socials and placed in concentration camps was much higher than in Fascist Italy.

The Nazi state intruded further into ordinary life than did its Italian counterpart. At the workplace Germans were increasingly influenced and controlled by the Nazi Labour Front, while their children were subject to indoctrination at school and pressurised into joining the Hitler Youth. Nazism even tried to attack traditional religious beliefs by setting up its own National Reich Church which hoped to replace the Cross and the Bible with a sword and a copy of *Mein Kampf*.

Mussolini, of course, also attempted to control, transform and militarise his people and employed similar methods, but he met with less success. Differences between German and Italian society help to explain why the Duce faced a more difficult task. The strong, authoritarian government established after unification in 1871 had demanded the loyalty of Germans and offered social stability, a heady, nationalistic foreign policy and a fairly comprehensive system of social and welfare benefits in return. Many Germans, particularly among the upper and middle classes, eagerly supported this regime and welcomed the rapid economic growth it brought with it. Germans, then, were accustomed to a disciplined society and used to a government which stressed the importance of the military. Furthermore, economic growth led to the development of excellent communications links within Germany and permitted a great expansion of state education. The Nazis benefited from this habit of obedience to the state and used the national media and agencies of the state, such as schools, to spread and enforce the Nazi message. In such an advanced industrialised society, it was easier to disseminate new ideas and to identify and eradicate opposition.

Italy, in contrast, possessed no such tradition of popular obedience to a strong government. The Liberal regime had struggled to impose its will on the new state and had not extended the role of government as far as its German counterpart. Italy remained a country where central government was viewed with great suspicion. Commands from Rome were often ignored, particularly in the south. Italy remained poor, despite the economic growth at the turn of the century. As a result Liberal governments were permanently short of money and were unable to fund an extension of state education properly or to improve the lamentable state of Italian communications. Fascist ideas could be spread with ease in the cities and towns of the more prosperous parts of northern Italy, but in large areas of the south, where illiteracy and poverty were prevalent, the peasants remained largely ignorant of the Duce's great plans for his country.

The existence within Italy of a powerful Catholic Church also limited the influence of Fascism. Mussolini's need for catholic support forced him to hide his own anti-clericalism and to conclude a Concordat guaranteeing the independence of the Church and permitting the continued existence of catholic schools. During the 1930s Mussolini tried to intimidate the Church over such issues as the catholic youth movement, but he never felt able to batter the Church into submission. For the Duce there was no possibility of creating a rival Fascist Church on the Nazi model.

The dictatorships differed not only in the degree of power they exerted over their respective societies, but also in one crucial part of their ideology. This was Hitler's obsession – the question of race. The

Führer's determination to create a 'master race' of pure Aryans decisively influenced both his domestic and foreign policies. If the master race was to come into existence then 'race defectives' must be removed and the *untermenschen* or sub-humans subjugated. Within Germany this justified the murder of thousands of the mentally and physically handicapped, and the systematic persecution of the Jews. In foreign policy this justified the racial war against the Slavs in the east and the genocide practised against the European Jews. Hitler had never disguised his anti-Semitism – *Mein Kampf* was littered with references to the Jews. By 1939 he could tell the Reichstag:

> If the international Jewish financiers in and outside Europe should succeed in plunging the nations into a world war, then the result will not be bolshevization of the earth and thus the victory of Jewry, but the annihilation of the Jewish race in Europe.

Hitler took his obsession to the grave. Writing his final will and testament in 1945 he stated:

> Above all, I demand of the nation's leaders and followers scrupulous adherence to the race laws and to ruthless resistance against the world poisoners of all peoples, international Jewry.

The Duce did not share this obsession. Mussolini believed that Italians had an innate superiority over other peoples but he never developed a racial ideology to underpin Italian Fascism. He did introduce anti-Jewish laws in the late 1930s but this action seems to have been prompted by pressure from his new ally in foreign policy adventures, Adolf Hitler. In fact, the Duce's anti-semitism, to the extent that it genuinely existed at all, developed very late in the day. He had told one interviewer in 1932:

> Anti-Semitism does not exist in Italy. Italians of Jewish birth have shown themselves good citizens and they fought bravely in the war. Many of them occupy leading positions in the universities, the army and the banks.

The Italian racial laws caused great hardship, but, unlike their German counterparts, the vast majority of Italian Jews avoided the Nazi death camps.

The Nazi racial ideology sponsored the growth of the SS, supposedly a pure Aryan elite. Conceived as an ultra-loyal bodyguard to the Führer, the SS grew in power, particularly during the Second World War. It formed its own very well equipped military units, administered large areas of the conquered territories in the east, and controlled the death camps. Italian Fascism possessed no such organisation. The blackshirt militia lacked energy and leadership. Where it did take part in military action, notably in the Spanish Civil War, it was singularly unsuccessful. Mussolini, for all his talk of the Fascist revolution, had little interest in the blackshirts once he had secured power.

8 Fascism and Spain

While many historians have been eager to point out the similarities between the Italian and German regimes there has been less agreement over the extent to which General Franco's Spain was modelled on either Mussolini's or Hitler's dictatorships. Those historians who have questioned whether there were any meaningful similarities between Spain and the two Fascist regimes have concentrated their attention on the character and style of Franco himself, and on the various political groups making up the regime.

Franco was certainly a very different character from both Mussolini and Hitler. In background he was not an outsider as the others had been. While Mussolini and Hitler struggled to make a mark in adult society, living on occasions as tramps, Franco was carving out for himself a military career. He had entered the Officers' Academy at the age of 14 and, once he had completed his training, his promotion had been rapid and assured. He was a career officer, a member of no political party, a man who saw civilian politics as too often petty and corrupt. Franco's political beliefs were little different from those of his fellow officers – conservative, authoritarian, and anti-socialist. He appears to have been a monarchist who was nevertheless prepared to give the Spanish Second Republic a chance to prove itself. Unlike Mussolini and Hitler, he was not driven by a burning desire to win political power. Only when he became convinced that the government had lost control in the streets and that a socialist-communist revolution was imminent did he join the military conspirators of 1936.

When the attempted coup began in July 1936 Franco was only one of its four possible leaders. In fact, Franco's lack of personal charisma and his inability to make inspiring, emotional speeches, seemed to suggest that he was not the man to lead the revolt. That Franco was appointed commander-in-chief of the armed forces and head of the rebel government (Generalissimo) in September 1936 was the result of fortuitous circumstances: the three rival generals were either dead, imprisoned by the republican government, or politically unacceptable to the right-wing parties supporting the revolt. And since the war was clearly going to last for some time, the rebels needed a leader of proven military experience and organisational ability.

As the rebel leader, Franco tried to bring all the anti-Republican forces together into a National Movement. The Falange, the one political party which was clearly and openly Fascist, formed only one part of this movement. The coalition also contained large numbers of conservative monarchists and Carlists, a group of militant catholics. The Falange, which had only become a major party during the troubles of 1936, was forced to compete with these other groups for influence. The party's task was made more difficult by the fact that it lacked leadership (its energetic leader, Jose Antonio Primo de Rivera, had been executed by Republicans) and because its ideas held only a limited attraction for the Generalissimo.

Franco shared the Falange's hatred of Marxism and agreed that independent trade unions should be suppressed, but he was unconvinced by the idea that Spanish society and industry needed a radical, modernising transformation. He was also unwilling to allow the Falange to form themselves into a genuine mass movement, since such a movement might challenge his own power. Franco's vision of Spain was conservative, and rather backward-looking. He stressed the importance of leadership, authority, discipline, religion and the family. Spain must restore these old virtues and resist contamination from foreign ideas, principally Marxism and liberalism.

The influence of the Falange, then, was limited and did not rival that of the Catholic Church. The accommodation between the regime and the Church in Spain was not the result of cynical political calculation, as it had been in Germany and Italy, but was a genuine alliance. The conflicts between regime and Church which arose in Germany and Italy had no parallel in Franco's Spain. The Church controlled Spanish education, the Jesuits were readmitted to the country, and all military and civilian officials were obliged to attend Mass regularly. The political importance of the Church in Spain was clearly recognised by Hitler. In fact, the Führer described Franco's regime as consisting principally of 'clerico-monarchical scum'.

This close alliance with the Church has, for some historians, confirmed that Franco's Spain had little in common with the German and Italian dictatorships. Indeed, the absence of charismatic leadership, the fact that the Falange was never the sole 'official' party of the regime, and the lack of interest in foreign adventures or in the radical transformation of society, have all been cited as evidence that Spain was never truly Fascist.

These differences between Spain and the Italian and German regimes were certainly marked. Nevertheless, there were some distinct parallels. Like Mussolini and Hitler, Franco wanted total power for himself. The General made himself head of state, head of the government, leader of the National Movement and commander of the armed forces. He appointed and dismissed all ministers and was responsible to no parliament or elected assembly. All opposition political parties were banned.

To maintain and increase his power, Franco played off the various groups within the National Movement against one another in much the same way as the Duce had done when dealing with conservatives and more radical Fascists both before and after 1922. In the absence of a clear ideology, Franco himself, like Mussolini, defined what the Movement stood for at any one time. As Franco changed his mind, so the official doctrine would change.

Franco also directly copied Italian Fascism in a number of respects. Recognising the political value of a cult of personality, he attempted to create one for himself. Styling himself *Caudillo*, a Spanish Duce, he posed as the firm yet benevolent leader of his country and as the man who had saved the nation from the 'red threat'. Impressed by the supposed success of Italian experiments in developing a corporate state, he allowed the Falange to create a Spanish imitation. Independent trade unions were suppressed and new state-controlled unions comprising employers, workers and state officials were set up. However, the Spanish 'Labour Organisation' was as ineffective as its Italian counterpart. In both Spain and Italy the state backed the employer and crushed any worker dissent.

Franco's intolerance of dissent extended beyond the banning of political parties and trade unions. Censorship was imposed on the press and on the arts. The state, guided by the Catholic Church, banned supposedly subversive books and magazines, decided which films could be shown in Spanish cinemas, and harried undesirable painters and musicians. In education, syllabuses were rewritten and school teachers deemed disloyal were dismissed.

Franco's determination to crush potential opposition therefore matched that of his fellow dictators and his methods suggested that he also shared something of their brutality. Having finally secured victory in the Civil War in early 1939, he wreaked his revenge on the losers. Thousands of so-called reds were executed, thousands more were imprisoned and 50,000 were forced into exile. It has been estimated that some 200,000 Spaniards died during this period of Francoist retribution.

If there were such parallels between Franco's and Mussolini's regimes, can Spain, after all, be described as the third Fascist regime in western Europe? The answer depends on the reader's definition of the meaning of Fascism. In the absence of a Fascist equivalent of the *Communist Manifesto* or *Das Kapital*, it has been particularly difficult for historians to agree on a definition. To those who emphasise the mass popular appeal of Fascist leaders, their attempted militarisation of society, their expansionism in foreign policy, and their hostility to organised religion, Franco's Spain was not a Fascist state. To those who adopt a more limited definition concentrating on Fascism's hatred of socialism and democracy, its intolerance of dissent, and its interest in a corporative state, Franco's Spain may be described as Fascist. It might also be useful to remember that most contemporaries engaged in the war against Franco's forces believed they were fighting against Fascism. As the British historian Martin Blinkhorn has remarked, 'if "Fascism" appeared to them an appropiate name for their enemy, then perhaps comfortable historians half a century later should hesitate before declaring them wrong'.

Making notes on 'Mussolini and the Fascist Political System'

This chapter has two distinct halves, one examining the nature of Mussolini's political system and the other discussing what Fascist Italy, Nazi Germany and Francoist Spain had in common. Your notes should reflect this division.

As you re-read the second half of the chapter be on the look out for answers to the question, 'Why have the three countries examined often been described as Fascist dictatorships?'

The following headings, sub-headings and questions should help you when making your notes:

1. Mussolini's aim: personal dictatorship. How did he achieve this?
2. Cult of Personality. What was its purpose? How did the regime propagate this cult?
2.1 How successful was the cult of personality?
3. Mussolini and government. How did he try to secure control over institutions of government? Did he succeed?
4. Mussolini and the Fascist party. How and why did he try to tame the party?
4.1 Party membership. Who became Fascists and why?
5. Relationship between party and state. How did they come into conflict? What were the consequences for Mussolini's power? How efficient was Mussolini's government? Why?
6. Popular support and opposition. How did he deter opposition and attract support? How successful was he?
7. Comparison between Italian Fascism and German Nazism. Similarities in the rise to power of Mussolini and Hitler.
7.1 Similarities and differences between the regimes, and the reasons for them.
8. Fascism and Spain. Similarities and differences between Franco's and Mussolini's regimes.

Answering essay questions on 'Mussolini and the Fascist Political System'

Examination papers often contain questions asking you to compare and contrast the Fascist regimes in Italy, Germany, and Spain. However, many students are very reluctant to tackle such questions. For some this is because they have 'compartmentalised' their knowledge and understanding of each of the countries they have studied and have neglected to identify or to think about themes that are common to several European countries in the same period. Avoid this pitfall if you possibly can. Otherwise you may rule yourself out from answering the questions set on the topics for which you have particularly prepared yourself. But for others it is simply that they lack the confidence to attempt what they think of as such 'hard' questions. This is a pity because comparisons of regimes are not as difficult as they appear. The key to success is to have worked out a general strategy for answering such questions before you enter the examination room. You should then not find it too difficult to adapt your approach to the wording of the question actually set.

Most questions ask you to compare either the growth and success of Fascism in Italy, Germany and Spain or the nature of the Fascist regimes in these countries. Examples of the two approaches are:

1. Compare Fascism's rise to power in Italy and Spain.
and,
2. Compare the regimes of the Duce and the Führer.

As you can see, the phrasing of such questions is usually very straightforward. This is another good reason for attempting these comparison-type questions if you possibly can.

The most common mistake made by candidates when answering questions such as question 1 is to spend half the essay explaining why Mussolini came to power and then to spend the second half explaining how Franco came to power. This normally results in the topic of the question being written about, rather than the question being answered directly, and in a maximum of half marks being gained.

If you are to tackle comparison questions really successfully, it is essential that you identify similarities and differences – in this case between the rise of Fascism in Italy and Spain – before you begin to write your essay. The simplest way to do this is to make a list of the reasons why Mussolini came to power and then to do the same for Franco. Now compare the two lists. Are there any common factors? Fear of a left-wing revolution, for example? List the common factors on a separate piece of paper, along with a few phrases to explain each factor and its significance. Now try to identify factors peculiar to each country and list these on a separate piece of paper. Read both pieces of paper again and decide whether or not the main reasons for Mussolini's and Franco's success are listed on the common factor sheet. Your decision will dictate the shape of your essay. For example, you might begin your essay by saying 'Widening political divisions exacerbated by economic problems fatally weakened the fragile democracies of both Italy and

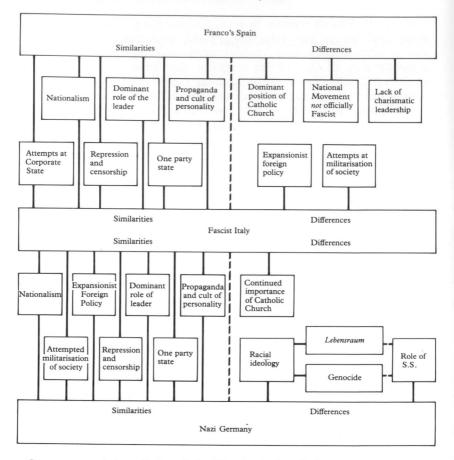

Summary – Mussolini and the Fascist Political System

Spain . . .' – such an opening signals to the examiner that you have decided that the common factors are of most importance. Most of the rest of your essay will be devoted to explaining what these common factors were and why they were so significant. Towards the end of your essay you should briefly discuss the role of factors peculiar to each country. What would your approach be if you decided that the common factors were less important than those that were particular to each country?

Now carry out the same process with the second question.

Source-based questions on 'Mussolini and the Fascist Political System'

1 Cult of Personality

Carefully examine the photographs on pages 74, 75, 76 and 77. Answer the following questions:

  a) What aspects of the Cult of Personality are illustrated by the photograph of Mussolini in Rome? (*4 marks*)
  b) The draining of the Pontine marshes to provide agricultural land for peasants was widely publicised by the Fascist government. What was the propaganda value of the photograph showing Mussolini in the Pontine marshes? (*4 marks*)
  c) Examine the photographs showing Mussolini at the harvest and with violin. Who were the intended audiences for this propaganda? Explain your answer. (*5 marks*)
  d) The four photographs are propaganda. Does this mean that they are of little use to the historian? Explain your answer. (*6 marks*)
  e) Why was Mussolini determined to develop a cult of personality? (*6 marks*)

2 The Dictators' Political Style

Carefully read William Shirer's impressions of a Nazi rally, Mussolini's reflections on Fascism's 'style', and the accounts of Mussolini's and Hitler's speech-making abilities on pages 85 and 86. Answer the following questions:

  a) What explanation does Shirer give of Hitler's success in conveying his ideas to the German people? (*4 marks*)
  b) What is Shirer's opinion of the Nazis? (*2 marks*)
  c) What is Mussolini's opinion of the Italian public? Explain your answer. (*3 marks*)
  d) How, and to what extent, did Italian Fascism bring back 'colour, force, picturesqueness, the unexpected, mysticism'? (*8 marks*)
  e) In what ways did the dictators' political styles, particularly Mussolini's, strengthen their regimes? (*8 marks*)

CHAPTER 6

Mussolini, the Economy, and Society

1 Mussolini's Aims

Mussolini, like Hitler, was neither an economist nor a deep or original thinker about social affairs. He did not come to power with a coherent programme. In fact, he had given little real thought to what he would do once in office. He had little knowledge of, or interest in the workings of the economy, while his policies towards society developed rather slowly and were rarely properly planned in advance.

Mussolini was determined to hang on to power and therefore, in his early years in office, he adopted policies that would make his position secure. His primary aim was to make the Duce all-powerful, but as the 1920s progressed he also revealed a desire to transform Italian society and even the Italian character. He wanted Italy to be militarily strong, playing a major role in European affairs, and carving herself an Empire to rival that of Ancient Rome. Such an Italy would need an economy capable of building and maintaining a modern war machine and would require a population of tough, disciplined and warlike citizens. Mussolini's preoccupations meant that the country's 'old problems' – industrial underdevelopment, rural poverty, the north-south divide, and illiteracy – were largely ignored. They were only tackled with any determination if they were obstacles to the achievement of the Duce's principal aims.

2 Economy

a) Industry

Mussolini was lucky enough to come to power just as Italian industry was beginning a period of 'boom'. The economic climate throughout Europe was improving and many Italian companies were able to sell their products abroad with ease. Indeed, exports, particularly of cars, textiles, and agricultural produce, doubled in the period 1922–5.

The new political regime claimed the credit for increasing company profits and attempted to win over the support of industrialists by appointing an economics professor, de Stefani, as treasury minister. De Stefani's orthodox, liberal economic policy limited government spending, thus lowering inflation, and reduced state intervention in industry. The telephone network was taken out of government control and handed back to private companies, while taxes levied on industries which had made huge profits from government contracts during the First World War were either reduced or abandoned. Industrialists were also pleased by the outlawing of socialist trade unions by the Vidoni Pact (see page 80) of 1925.

* However, after 1925 Mussolini began to take less notice of business interests. The dismissal of de Stefani and the revaluation of the Italian currency were two early but important examples of this. Revaluation was particularly significant. By the mid 1920s the exchange rate of the lire was around 150 to the pound, a rate Mussolini found unacceptable. He considered that a strong, vibrant country should have a strong, vibrant currency and, consequently, in 1927 he decided to try to set a new rate of exchange of 90 lire to the pound. This decision increased Mussolini's prestige both with foreign financiers and with the Italian public, and thus the Duce's main aim had been achieved. But, the effects on the Italian economy were far from beneficial. At a stroke, foreign buyers found Italian goods nearly twice as expensive, and it was not surprising that Italian export industries, particularly textiles, went into depression. Even Fiat was exporting fewer cars in the late 1930s than it had done in the early 1920s.

The revaluation of the lire should have helped the Italian consumer because imports of foods and other products from abroad should have become cheaper. However, the Duce prevented this by placing high tariffs on many foreign imports. The only winners in economic terms were those industries such as steel, armaments and ship building which needed large supplies of cheap tariff-free imported raw materials. It was these heavy industries that would be promoted throughout Fascist rule. They made healthy profits from the protected domestic market while export industries were neglected.

* The early 1930s saw a worldwide economic depression and Italy did not escape its effects. A large number of companies collapsed and unemployment rose to two million by 1933. The democratic governments of western Europe and the USA were reluctant to intervene to help the private sector out of its difficulties as their traditional economic philosophy regarded such actions as being counter-productive. The Italian fascist state had no such qualms. It introduced public works schemes, notably building motorways and hydro-electric power plants, which put the unemployed back to work with money in their pockets. The state also did much to avoid the banking collapse which affected the USA and Germany in particular. Banks had lent money to industry, but as many companies could no longer meet the repayments on their loans banks found themselves without enough money to pay their investors. The fascist government simply stepped in and 'bailed out' the banks.

A result of this intervention was the creation of the Institute for Industrial Reconstruction (IRI) in January 1933. This efficiently run organisation took over from the banks the responsibility for providing loans for Italian industry. It also attempted to promote the latest managerial techniques, with some success.

The government's measures may have cost the taxpayer a great deal of money, but they did enable Italy to weather the depression a little

better than her democratic neighbours. Indeed, Mussolini was delighted to hear his admirers claim that President Roosevelt had copied the
Duce's example when drawing up America's 'New Deal'.

* Mussolini's economic policies had never been designed simply to
increase the wealth of the country or the prosperity of the ordinary
Italian, and this became very apparent by the mid 1930s. As the
Dictator became increasingly pre-occupied with foreign affairs, living
standards and the general welfare of the economy suffered. He believed
that war, either in Europe or to further his African Empire, was almost
inevitable and that Italy must be prepared. The armaments industries
must be promoted, and Italy's economy must become self-sufficient.
Italy should be an autarky – able to supply itself with all the food and
material needed to fight a modern war. The economic sanctions
imposed by the League of Nations after Italy's invasion of Ethiopia in
1935 seemed to prove his point that there must be no reliance on
imports. Mussolini therefore encouraged heavy industries such as steel,
chemicals, and shipbuilding by placing large government contracts.
State control was expanded to the point where 80 per cent of
shipbuilding and 50 per cent of steel production was directed by the
government. Economies of scale were looked for and the regime
allowed major companies to merge into near monopoly organisations.
Fiat, for instance, controlled car manufacturing, while Pirelli dominated rubber, and Montecatini chemicals. Exports, as usual, took low
priority.

Despite these efforts the Italian economy was still far from self-
sufficient when the Duce declared war in 1940, and indeed it had run
into major difficulties. The huge sums of money required for rearmament and adventures in Ethiopia and Spain could not be raised simply
by increasing taxes, and the government found that its expenditure was
greater than its income. Massive budget deficits had arisen by the late
1930s for which the remedy was either swingeing cuts in military
expenditure or very significant reductions in living standards. Typical-
ly, Mussolini refused to recognise the seriousness of the economic
situation and the problem remained unsolved when Italy entered the
Second World War.

* How did the industrial workers fare under fascism? After all,
fascism was supposed to eliminate the struggles between employer and
employee which had led to strikes and riots in pre-fascist Italy. Class
conflict was to be a thing of the past. The various classes should work
together harmoniously for the good of the nation. The worker should
no longer be 'exploited' and should be able to look forward to greater
prosperity and increased respect within society.

At first, the workers benefited from the economic revival of the early
1920s. Unemployment fell and de Stefani's policies curbed inflation.
Admittedly, the years 1925 and 1926 saw the banning of independent
trade unions and the abolition of the right to strike, but Mussolini

claimed to be about to transform the Italian economy. The new 'corporative system' would involve setting up trade unions consisting of both employers and employees. Each trade union, or corporation, would organise production and working conditions in its own industry. Since, in Mussolini's view, both employers and employees would be dedicated fascists they would agree on the best policy to pursue. In fact, he even hoped that parliament would be replaced by an assembly of these corporations, representing all the types of industry in Italy.

A Ministry of Corporations was set up in 1926 and within three years it claimed to have removed all class conflict in industry. However, what had happened in reality was that the employees were unable to choose their own representatives in their corporation, and instead had fascist nominees foisted upon them. These fascist officials tended to side with the employers' representatives. Industrialists kept their power and independence. In truth, the 'corporative revolution' never materialised. Conflict between employer and employee was not solved, only suppressed, and the corporations never achieved the pivotal role in the state and the economy envisaged by the Duce.

Workers had lost their freedoms and their standard of living was about to decline seriously. As the economic revival petered out in the late 1920s, industry responded by lengthening working hours and abandoning the eight hour day. Wages were also cut. It is estimated that during the period 1925–38 real wages for the Italian worker fell by over 10 per cent. At the same time, unemployment began to rise, despite the public works programmes, and totalled some two million by 1933. This was a figure close to that of Britain, after allowing for the difference in populations. The British 'Hungry Thirties' were paralleled in Italy. Even Mussolini recognised this and dropped his claims that he had improved the workers' lot. Instead, by December 1930 he was saying:

fortunately the Italian people were not accustomed to eat much and therefore feel the privation less than others.

And, by 1936, he was arguing that:

We must rid our minds of the idea that what we have called the days of prosperity may return. We are probably moving toward a period when humanity will exist on a lower standard of living.

The Duce had never really been committed to raising the standard of living of ordinary Italians and viewed economic hardship as by no means a bad thing for his people.

b) Agriculture

Mussolini did not concern himself with the underlying problems of Italian agriculture – the existence of a sizeable class of poor, land-hungry peasants and the use of backward, inefficient farming methods. Instead, as with industry, he occupied himself with projects which would either increase his personal power and prestige or else supposedly help Italy become a self-sufficient state in case of war.

The Dictator's first major scheme was the 'Battle for Grain'. It began in 1925 and attempted to achieve both aims. Traditionally, Italy had needed to import large quantities of grain in order to feed her people. Mussolini saw this as a grave weakness, as in time of war supplies could be cut off and the country would face starvation. A campaign to increase grain production dramatically would solve this problem and would also illustrate to the world just how dynamic the new fascist state could be. Consequently, the government offered grants to enable farmers to buy tractors, fertilisers, and other machinery necessary for wheat production. Free advice was made available on the latest, efficient farming techniques. Farmers were also guaranteed a high price for the grain they produced.

The incentives did work and the average harvest rose from 5.5 million tonnes per year in the early 1920s to over seven million tonnes ten years later. Grain imports declined sharply. The Battle for Grain appeared to be a resounding success and Mussolini claimed the credit. He ensured that press photographers were on hand to record him visiting farms and helping out with the harvest. Not only was the Duce a genius for conceiving the Battle for Grain, he was also prepared to get his hands dirty in the fields – a true leader of his people! Appearances, however, were deceptive.

The Battle for Grain certainly had dramatically increased production and helped farmers, but there had been a large price to be paid. Firstly, much of the land in the central and southern regions which had been turned over to wheat was unsuitable for such a crop. The soil conditions and hotter, drier climate were more suited to the growing of citrus fruits or the production of wine and olive oil. The result was that these traditional agricultural exports declined. Furthermore, Italian consumers had to pay more for their bread as the result of government taxes and a tariff on imported grain.

Fascism's second major initiative, and an equally highly publicised one, was land reclamation and improvement. Liberal governments had made a start here, providing money to drain or irrigate farmland. Mussolini simply expanded these schemes. The Pontine Marshes, only 50 kilometres from Rome and handy for foreign pressmen, were the showpiece. These malarial swamps were drained and a network of small farms was set up, owned by ex-servicemen. Overall, land reclamation was a success, as much because it improved public health and provided thousands of jobs during the Depression. The amount of land reclaimed was, however, very limited.

* Of course, rural poverty was just as widespread as ever, particularly in the south. This poverty was worsened by the USA's decision to stop virtually all further immigration. In the first two decades of the century 200,000 Italians, mainly southerners, had emigrated to the USA each year. With this escape route from rural poverty closed, more Italians left the countryside for the towns and cities to find work and a better standard of living. Up to half a million people left the land in the 1920s and 1930s, despite the fact that Mussolini tried to prevent all further migration. He claimed to have a love for the countryside and wanted to 'ruralise' Italy, creating a vigorous class of prosperous peasants devoted to fascism. However, his government did nothing to bring this about. In fact, his policies brought much more benefit to large landowners than to poor and landless peasants. Such peasants needed enough land to support their families: a law to break up big estates and to distribute them to the peasants had been introduced into parliament in 1922, but Mussolini quietly dropped the policy for fear of offending the great landowners, his political supporters.

3 Society

Mussolini wanted to see Fascism penetrate every aspect of Italian society, but he was neither systematic in his ideas nor prepared to force through policies that might make him unpopular. His realisation that Fascism must compromise in order to secure support was particularly evident in his dealings with the Church.

* Mussolini never lost the anti-religious attitudes of his youth, but he was shrewd enough to realise that an accommodation with the Catholic Church could bring him great public support and increase the prestige of his regime abroad. As early as 1921 he told the Chamber of Deputies,

1 I affirm in this House that the Latin tradition of Imperial Rome is today represented by Catholicism . . . I am very much disturbed when I see churches being founded on a national basis because it means that millions and millions of men will no longer look
5 towards Italy and towards Rome. And this is why I advance this hypothesis: I believe that, should the Vatican definitely give up its temporal dreams, Italy should afford the Vatican all material help and encouragement for its schools, its churches, its hospitals or any other pious and civil manifestation. Because the development
10 of Catholicism in the world, an increase in the four hundred million men who look towards Rome from all parts of the earth, is of interest and a source of pride for us Italians.

By the time he became prime minister in 1922 Mussolini was posing as an alternative to anti-catholic Liberals and 'godless' communists and socialists. Restoring catholic education in state schools and increasing government payments to priests secured the confidence of the Pope who, in 1923, withdrew his support for the *Popolari*, the catholic political party. These moves neutralised, at least temporarily, the Church as a potential source of opposition. However, it did not mean that fascism had the active support of the Vatican – this would only come with the Lateran Agreement of 1929.

The treaty and concordat which comprised the Lateran Agreement ended the conflict between Church and state that had existed since the foundation of the Italian kingdom in 1870. In the treaty, the Pope agreed to recognise the Italian state and its possession of Rome and the old Papal States. In return, the state recognised the Pope's sovereignty over the Vatican City. The Pope also received financial compensation of £30 million for surrendering his claim to Rome. The Concordat established catholicism as the state religion of Italy and outlined what this would mean in practice: the Pope could appoint all bishops, but the government could veto any politically suspect candidates; the state would pay the salaries of the clergy; clergy could not belong to political parties; religious education, of a catholic nature, would be compulsory in state schools; there would be no divorce without the consent of the Church and civil marriage would no longer be required by law.

The Lateran Agreement signalled that Mussolini had given up any hope of removing the influence of catholicism from Italian society. Nevertheless, he was very happy with the deal. Clerics could not become a focus of opposition and, more importantly, the Church would throw its support behind Mussolini as Duce. As the American *Time* magazine reported in 1929:

1 Leaning forward in a carved armchair at the Palazzo Chigi, Signor
   Benito Mussolini sat with his hard chin cupped between con-
   tented palms watching newsreel flashes of Cardinals and Monsig-
   nors marching to the ballot box, attended by blaring brass bands
5 and wildly cheering throngs. Never before have Princes of the
   Church shepherded their clergy and people to vote in a Parliamentary Election of the present Italian Kingdom. Always
   before the priesthood has abstained, urging their flocks to do
   likewise, in protest against the Government's suppression of the
10 Pope's temporal power in 1870. Recently, however, 'Il Duce' has
   restored a mite of earthly authority to 'Il Papa' and last week
   cinema machines proved how mountainous is the Pontiff's grati-
   tude to the Dictator. Especially vivid were the footages showing
   Cardinal La Fontaine, Patriarch of Venice; Cardinal Gamba,
15 Archbishop of Turin; and Cardinal Maffi, Archbishop of Pisa, all
   of whom proceeded directly from the celebration of High Mass to
   vote at the head of their clergy. Pollsters estimated that His

Holiness' influence had flung into the scale of 'Fascismo' at least
1,000,000 extra votes. Last week's election statistics prove that
20 those Italians who went to the polls are 98.28% pure endorsers of
the 'Duce' – a record eclipsed in the U.S. only by Ivory Soap.

The Lateran Agreement was hailed as a great achievement, but not
all Italians were impressed. The exiled intellectual G.A. Borgese
attempted to explain why the Church had reached such an accommodation with Fascism and outlined what he saw as the consequences:

1 There was no reason why Pope and Duce, whom a parallel
destiny had brought in the same year to Rome, should not come
together: no reason except in Christ; but Christianism was by no
means the most decisive factor in Pope Ratti's mind. He was sure
5 that he loved Italy; it is sure that he hated democracy and
Socialism . . . the ruthless anti-christianity of Fascism, which
would have horrified a Francis or a Savonarola, was nothing to
him.
    The Church became ancillary to atheistic tyranny, and tyranny
10 rewarded it by making it supreme in the elementary cell of
society, the family. Marriage and divorce became a monopoly of
the Vatican, and the priest lent his hand to the squadrist in the
task of perverting domestic virtues to the purpose of national
violence and international anarchy. The intellectual life of the
15 country, already agonizing in the gas chamber of Fascist censorship, had its coup de grace from the spirit of the Inquisition,
and over her new black shirt Italy donned her old black gown.

However, the 'love affair' between catholicism and Fascism was not a
smooth one and it cooled as Mussolini increasingly tried to shape
society into a fascist mould. The first open dispute between Church and
state came in 1931 when the government attempted to suppress the
Church-sponsored 'Catholic Action'. This body provided a rival to
fascism's own youth and leisure organisations. A compromise was
reached confining youth groups within Catholic Action to purely
religious activities, but the mistrust remained.
    Senior clergy did support Italian involvement in the wars in Ethiopia
and Spain as they saw them as 'Christian Crusades', spreading and
defending the faith, but they were critical of the general trend of fascist
policy. The creed of the fascist Balilla (see page 107) was declared
blasphemous and Mussolini's racial policy was opposed from the start.
The Duce had never shared Hitler's obsessive hatred of the Jews, but
he felt pressured to show 'fascist solidarity' with his new ally. He
therefore adopted anti-semitic measures in 1938. Jews were banned
from teaching in state schools, forbidden to marry non-Jews, and
prevented from owning large companies or large landed estates.

Anti-semitism was never widespread either in Italian society or, indeed, within the fascist party, and these laws were never properly enforced. Nevertheless, the Pope, Pius XI, spoke out in protest. By 1939, the tacit alliance between catholicism and Fascism was over, and the Pope openly regretted the Church's earlier eagerness to embrace the Duce.

* One sphere of life where fascist policy and catholic belief could coincide was the role of the sexes. Catholicism held that birth control and abortion were unnatural and offensive to God, and implied that woman's role should be that of wife and mother. Mussolini was happy to ban contraception and to encourage women to have children, but for rather different reasons. The Duce's concern was to raise the population dramatically and so provide soldiers for his armies and colonists for the new Italian Empire.

A 'Battle for Births', launched in 1927, was designed to increase the population from 40 million to 60 million by 1950. Mussolini specified 12 children per family as the ideal. To achieve this a series of 'carrot and stick' measures was introduced. Marriage loans were offered to encourage couples to have more children. Part of the loan was cancelled as each new child was born. A further financial inducement was that a married man with at least six children was exempt from all taxation. Propaganda suggested that all good Italians had a duty to produce children for the Duce. Indeed, Mussolini gave prizes to the most prolific mothers.

For those still reluctant to become parents, penalties were introduced. Bachelors were taxed increasingly, to the point where the government raised some 230 million lire in 1939, and, by the late 1930s, jobs and promotions in the civil service were open only to the fertile married. Pressure was exerted on women to stay at home; private companies promoted married men, while the state railway company sacked all women who had been appointed since 1915, with the exception of war widows. Such discrimination was primarily designed to win the Battle for Births, but it also proved useful in coping with the unemployment problem.

Despite all the measures, and to Mussolini's mystification, the Battle for Births was lost. The rate of marriage remained unchanged, while the birth rate declined until 1936 and rose only slightly thereafter. Indeed, the 1936 figure of 102 live births per 1,000 women of child-bearing age compared very unfavourably with the 147 per 1,000 in 1911. As for the target population of 60 million by 1950, all the Duce's efforts could only produce 47.5 million Italians by this date. During the Second World War Mussolini reflected bitterly that Italians' lack of patriotic effort in this field had lost him the equivalent of 15 army divisions.

* Mussolini's dream of millions of aggressive, athletic, disciplined fascists spreading Italian power overseas led to his interest in the education and training of the young. He was also fully aware that loyal

youth could help preserve the regime both at the time and in the future. In schools the cult of personality was heavily promoted. Teachers were ordered to stress Mussolini's genius and were supplied with sycophantic biographies for use in the classroom. The Duce's portrait had to be hung alongside that of the king. Italian youth was to have absolute, unquestioning faith, as the compulsory textbook for eight-year-olds explained:

1 The eyes of the Duce are on every one of you. A child who, even while not refusing to obey, asks 'Why?' is like a bayonet made of milk. You must obey because you must. What is the duty of a child? Obedience! The second? Obedience! The third? Obedi-
5 ence!

Mussolini had been sent by providence to restore Italian greatness and students must learn to take pride in the Italian nation. Accordingly, History and Italian literature became priorities in schools. Existing books which were insufficiently patriotic were banned. In 1926 this amounted to 101 out of 317 History texts in schools and, by 1936, a single official text was compulsory. Students were to be left in no doubt that Italy had been the cradle of European civilisation and that Italians had always been at the forefront of events. After all, Marco Polo had been Italian, as had Michelangelo, and Christopher Columbus. According to the fascists it had been Italian victories in the First World War that had saved Britain, France, and the USA from defeat! Above all, under the guidance of the Duce, Italy would be restored to her rightful place in the world, as the creed of the fascist youth organisation made clear:

1 I believe in Rome the Eternal, the mother of my country, and in Italy her eldest daughter, who was born in her virginal bosom by the grace of God; who suffered through the barbarian invasions, was crucified and buried, who descended to the grave and was
5 raised from the dead in the nineteenth century, who ascended into heaven in her glory in 1918 and 1922. I believe in the genius of Mussolini, in our Holy Father Fascism, in the communion of its martyrs, in the conversion of Italians, and in the resurrection of the Empire.

Young people were to identify themselves with Mussolini, Fascism, and Italy and to see the three as inseparable. To build a new Italy, young people had to work together and see themselves as a group. Mussolini outlined this in 1932:

Here in Italy we educate them in accordance with the ideal of the nation, whereas in Russia children are brought up in accordance with the ideals of a class. Still, the ultimate aim is identical. Both in Italy and in Russia the individual is subordinate to the state.

Fascism was concerned not just with what happened at school, but was also determined to influence young people in their leisure time. The *Opera Nazionale Balilla* (ONB) was set up to organise youth movements and membership became compulsory for all children at state schools by the early 1930s. By 1937 over seven million had joined the ONB. The Fascist apologist Missiroli explained its aims, organisation, and activities:

1 It is a moral entity having as its objectives the assistance and moral and physical education of the youth of the country carried out by means of a continuous activity inside and outside the schools and intended to transform the Italian nation 'body and
5 soul'. The *Opera* performs its functions through the *Balilla* and *Avanguardisti* institutions. Children from 8 to 14 years old belong to the *Balilla* and the *Avanguardisti* include boys from 14 to 18 years of age. In respect of girls, the *Piccole Italiane* correspond to the *Balilla*, and the *Giovani Italiane* to the *Avanguardisti*.
10   It diffuses throughout all social stratas that training in arms which has restored to honour the virtue of courage, personal responsibility and initiative. Its action is far reaching, incessant and progressive. Instruction, gymnastics, sport, camping, cruises, military exercises, artistic and musical activities and
15 excursions all tend to create an atmosphere of equality, emulation, and solidarity which has not been achieved by any other institution in the world.

The Duce hoped that here would be his future soldiers.
* Despite all these efforts, Mussolini was not content to wait for youth to grow up and transform the Italian character. He sought to influence adult Italians there and then. Ordinary Italians had been tamed at work, through the banning of trade unions and by other fascist controls, and the regime tried to maintain this control outside the workplace. The *Dopolavoro* was set up in 1925 to provide leisure activities that would influence workers towards a fascist view of life and compensate for the now defunct trade union sponsored clubs.

The *Dopolavoro* organisation expanded quickly and by the mid-1930s controlled all soccer clubs, 1,350 theatres, 2,000 dramatic societies, 3,000 brass bands and 8,000 libraries. Virtually every town and village, even in the south, had its *Dopolavoro* clubhouse and membership had risen from 300,000 in 1926 to nearly 4 million in 1939. Coercing people into membership was rarely necessary as working-class Italians were quick to take advantage of subsidised sports, entertainments, excursions and holidays. The *Dopolavoro's* popularity was also due to the fact that only lip service was paid to fascist ideas of physical and military training. The emphasis was not on indoctrination, but on having a good time. The relative absence of propaganda can be illustrated by the programme of the theatre company *Carro di Tespi*. Of the seven plays performed in Rome in 1938, five were comedies or farces, and only two were serious plays, neither of which had any direct relevance to fascist ideology.

* If the *Dopolavoro* was a popular initiative, other fascist policies affecting ordinary people only lost support for the regime. The 1930s saw the attempted introduction of a range of initiatives and directives which appeared to most Italians as petty, interfering and ridiculous. For example, the fascist salute, a replacement for the handshake, was officially made compulsory in 1937, while in the following year Italians were told to stop using 'lei' the polite form of address and instead say 'voi', a word apparently more completely 'Italian' in derivation. Attempts were made to change the calendar so that Year 1 would be 1922, the year of the fascist seizure of power. Even fashion was subject to the whims of the Duce. Time magazine reported in 1929:

1 Acting in his capacity as Minister of the Interior, Il Duce notified all prefects of Italian provinces that 'beauty contests, with their consequent naming of "queens" and "princesses", lower the moral standard of communities and tend to dangerous exaltation
5 of feminine vanity as well as constituting a parody on very serious matters. Therefore, let there be no more beauty contests.' Correspondents in Rome learned other more practical reasons for the new prohibition. After two years of competing in these strange, international competitions, it has been noticed that Italy
10 invariably loses. Any competition in which Italy loses is not one to be encouraged by the Fascist State. 'Foreigners might get the impression,' explained a Black-shirt chieftain gravely, 'that there are no pretty girls in Italy!' Immediately following Prime Minister Mussolini's circular came an order from the Secretary General of
15 the Fascist party, Signor Augusto Turati. Last month he had ordered all 'young and even little' Italian girls to have their skirts at least two fingers' lengths below their knees. Last week he altered his order to apply to all females, regardless of age.

Eventually, fascism even tried to ban the wearing of trousers by women. Such rules were unenforceable and simply irritated Italians.

4 How far did Mussolini Achieve his Economic and Social Aims?

The Duce's principal aim was to maintain and increase his power, and his domestic policies did bring him substantial public support.

However, this support derived not from public recognition of real achievement, but from the effects of Fascist propaganda. Mussolini was constantly portrayed as an infallible genius, a man, even a superman, destined to lead Italy back to greatness. The Duce, so it was said, had a brilliant, original mind, but also appreciated the thoughts and needs of ordinary Italians, a claim emphasised by press photos of him helping out in the harvest and laying the foundations of some new building or *autostrada*. Fascist initiatives were apparently always great successes, such as the Battle for Grain and Land Reclamation, while Fascist failures such as the Battle for Births, were quietly forgotten.

Italians were not wholly taken in by this incessant stream of propaganda, but they were not averse to the Duce's claims that Italy possessed the greatest civilisation. They enjoyed Italian successes, such as victories in the 1934 and 1938 soccer World Cup and Primo Carnera's winning of the World Heavyweight Boxing Championship. The Duce, of course, claimed the credit. However, much of Mussolini's enhanced support derived from the apparent results of foreign policy. In fact, his concordat with the Catholic Church was perhaps his only real achievement of any note in the domestic sphere and even that was beginning to sour by the late 1930s.

Mussolini had hoped to transform the Italian character and Italian society into a fascist mould, but he was disappointed. The race of athletic, aggressive, obedient, fascists never materialised. Fascism did not penetrate the psyche of most Italians, changing traditional habits and attitudes. There was outward conformity but little inner conviction. Although Fascist propaganda claimed that it was transforming Italy, the reality was rather different. Fascism might claim, for example, to be creating a fascist youth via control of the school curriculum and the power of the ONB, but it is uncertain how many true converts there were. A substantial proportion left school at the age 11 and so avoided the full programme of indoctrination, while in private and catholic schools the state curriculum and ONB membership were never enforced.

Parents and the older generation were still more resistant to change, as they showed by their 'unpatriotic' reaction to the Battle for Births, and by their irritation at being told to adopt the new fascist salute, the new form of address and the instructions on what to wear. Fascist policies would be tolerated and even welcomed if they afforded some apparent advantage, such as *Dopolavoro* cheap holidays, but were resisted if they seemed to threaten entrenched customs and habits. Thus in the late 1930s, as Fascism tried to intrude further into everyday life, popular support for the regime began to decline. Furthermore, the Fascist government had neither the means nor the self-confidence to force through unpopular policies.

If Fascism did not dominate society, then neither did it dominate industry and agriculture, despite the claims that the corporate state had revolutionised relations between state, employer, and employee. Free trade unions had been smashed, but the employers' side of industry maintained its independence throughout. *Confindustria*, the industrialists' organisation, was never a hotbed of Fascism, but recognised the advantages of working with the regime. Indeed, several Presidents of *Confindustria* became ministers. These industrial barons, certainly those in heavy industry and armaments, enjoyed government contracts and the freedom to form near-monopoly organisations, but resisted party control and attempted state direction. Smaller firms were often the victims as industrial giants such as Fiat priced them out of the market.

In agriculture, too, the employers – in this case, the great landowners – maintained their power and wealth. The life of the peasant was as hard as it had ever been, as the migration from countryside to towns proved.

Mussolini's idea of autarky, of an Italy self-sufficient in industry and food and able to sustain itself in a major war, remained just a pipe-dream. Some progress was made by way of the Battle for Grain and through support for heavy industry, but Italy was never remotely self-sufficient. The Italian economy was not ready for war in 1940. Throughout the war the country was desperately short of coal, a crucial commodity for armaments industries, and was unable to match her enemies' levels of production. In fact, Italy could not even replace her losses in shipping and aircraft. However, in economic terms – despite the failure of autarky – the development of Italian industry and agriculture up to 1940 was not disastrous. Output did increase, and big companies did well. Nevertheless, Italy remained relatively backward compared to Germany, France and Great Britain. The Duce had made no serious effort to solve this problem, nor did he address himself to the other fundamental difficulties faced by his country. The north-south divide was as wide as ever, rural poverty probably deepened, and illiteracy levels remained depressingly high – 20 per cent in Italy as a whole, but 48 per cent in Calabria in the south. Only in the field of communications did Fascism make real progress, building *autostrada*, electrifying 5,000 km of railway line, and 'making the trains run on time', but it should be remembered that such improvements were made principally for propaganda purposes – their economic benefit would be felt only after the Second World War and the demise of Fascism. Mussolini had brought stability of a sort to Italy. He remained in power for 21 years, being personally popular for the greater part of this time, but he had not brought about a revolution.

The Second World War provided final proof of Mussolini's failure. Instead of his dream of a warlike, disciplined nation, enthusiastically fighting to restore Italian greatness and to prove the superiority of Fascism, the world witnessed a nation unable to cope with the demands of a modern war and quickly wearying of an apparently senseless struggle. From being perhaps the best loved man in Italy, Mussolini was, by 1943, certainly the most despised.

Making notes on 'Mussolini, the Economy, and Society'

Your notes on this chapter should form an analysis of (i) the motives behind Mussolini's domestic policies, (ii) the extent to which he achieved his aims, and (iii) the effect of his policies on Italian society. The following headings, sub-headings, and questions should help you.

1. General Aims.
2. De Stefani and early policy towards the economy.
2.1 Increasing intervention in the economy – revaluation of the lire.
2.2 The effects of the worldwide Depression. How did the regime attempt to deal with the Depression and with what success?
2.3 The drive for autarky. Why did Mussolini want autarky? What problems did the policy make worse?
2.4 Industrial workers. How did Fascist measures, such as the 'corporative system', affect employees?
2.5 Agriculture – Battle for Grain and Land Reclamation. What were the motives behind the policies and what were the results?
2.6 Rural Poverty and Migration.
3. Aims for Society.
3.1 Relations with the Church. Why did Mussolini seek an accommodation with the Catholic Church?
3.2 Battle for Births.
3.3 Education and the ONB.
3.4 *Dopolavoro*.
3.5 Fascism and everyday life.
4. Assessment: How far did Mussolini achieve his economic and social aims? How popular were the regime's domestic policies? What was the overall impact of Fascism on society and the economy?

Answering essay questions on 'Mussolini, the Economy, and Society'

Examination questions tend to concentrate on the impact of Fascism on Italian life, the revolutionary nature of Fascism, and the popular appeal of the regime. An example is:

1. To what extent did Fascism effect a revolution in Italy?

Clearly, such an essay requires a knowledge of policy towards the economy and society, but also needs an understanding of the Fascist political system and foreign policy.

The first thing to do is to consider what 'revolution' might mean in this context. A simple definition would be 'major change at a rapid pace', although you could come up with a range of definitions and test each one. You must then consider which, if any, aspects of Italian society were subject to a 'revolution' – the structure of government? – the style of government? – the economy? – everyday life? – foreign policy? Draw up and complete the following table:

	Major changes	Minor changes	No change
Government structure			
Government style			
Economy			
Other aspects . . .			

Once you have drawn up the table you should be in a position to decide on your line of argument. You might also consider whether the regime or people at the time believed a 'revolution' was taking place.

Other questions are variants on:

2. How popular was the fascist regime in the period 1922–40?

Again, you must break down the question. It is important to remember that different groups within society would have different opinions about the regime: make a list of the policies each group (eg. women, industrialists, and farmers) would like and a further list of those they wouldn't like. Then think about how opinions changed during the period – for instance, reactions to the Lateran Agreement or foreign adventures. Lastly, and on a more sophisticated level, consider the effects of propaganda on public opinion, the personal popularity of the Duce, and the difficulties in measuring how popular a government is, especially when there are no regular, free elections.

It is important to remember that essay questions on the Fascist regime often require knowledge not of the economy society during the period, but also of foreign policy and the system of government.

Summary – Mussolini, the Economy, and Society

Source-based questions on 'Mussolini, the Economy, and Society'

1 Fascism and the Catholic Church

Read carefully the three extracts on pages 103, 104, and 105. Answer the following questions:

    a) What, according to the first extract, is Mussolini's interest in the 'development of the Catholic Church'? (*4 marks*)

    b) What were the 'temporal dreams' of the Vatican referred to by Mussolini? (*4 marks*)

    c) How do *Time* magazine and Borgese explain the Pope's and Mussolini's interest in reaching an agreement? (*5 marks*)

d) '. . . a record eclipsed in the U.S. only by ivory soap'. What is the significance of this remark at the end of the *Time* report? (*4 marks*)

e) How accurate is Borgese's account of the relationship between Fascism and the Church after the Lateran Agreement? (*8 marks*)

2 Fascism and Young People

Read carefully the three extracts on pages 107 and 108. Answer the following questions:

a) According to Missiroli, page 108, what is the purpose of the ONB? (*5 marks*)

b) How far does the ONB, as described by Missiroli, accord with Mussolini's view of the proper role of education (page 107)? (*6 marks*)

c) Explain the phrase from the *Balilla* oath (page 107) that Italy 'was raised from the dead in the nineteenth century . . . (and) . . . ascended into heaven in her glory in 1918 and 1922.' (lines 5–6) (*6 marks*)

d) How far can the historian accept the argument, as outlined by Missiroli, that the ONB was a great success for Fascism? (*8 marks*)

CHAPTER 7

Mussolini and the Wider World

1 Mussolini's Aims

On coming to power in 1922 Mussolini did not have any clear foreign policy. It was apparent that he had completely rejected the anti-imperialist, anti-war beliefs of his youth, but it was uncertain how far he had adopted the views of his political allies, the nationalists. He had loudly supported entry into the First World War and had condemned the peace settlement – the 'mutilated victory' – but it was unclear what treaty revisions he would seek.

There was no foreign policy 'master plan', but in his first few months in office the new prime minister did begin to develop a general aim – in his words, 'to make Italy great, respected, and feared'. Italy would achieve great power status via military build-up, diplomatic intrigue and, if need be, war. She would one day be the dominant power in the Mediterranean, would develop and even expand her colonial empire in Africa, and would have the Balkans as her own sphere of influence. The Duce would be the architect of all this and would have transformed the Italians into a more energetic and aggressive people in the process.

However, until the 1930s these plans lacked detail. Mussolini was not sure which colonies would expand. Nor did he know how he would achieve 'dominance' in the Mediterranean, or how much power he desired in the Balkans. Nevertheless, the Duce's overall objectives remained the same, even if circumstances, particularly the general situation in Europe, would force him to adopt a variety of tactics in pursuing these objectives.

The Duce soon recognised that foreign affairs could provide him with the ideal stage – he would impress his fellow-countrymen with spectacles where he would overshadow foreign statesmen and defend and promote Italian interests with unending success. He would conduct foreign policy himself, avoiding the old, stuffy foreign office, and reap international prestige and internal support. Foreign affairs would take up more and more of his time.

Mussolini appears to have convinced himself that he was beginning a new era in Italian foreign policy. In truth, desire for great power status, high military expenditure, and colonial adventures had also been a feature of the Liberal regime, particularly under Crispi. However, Mussolini exceeded his Liberal predecessors in his ambitions and pursued his goals more relentlessly and recklessly, particularly in the 1930s. He squandered vast sums on colonial conflicts, and led Italy into a disastrous world war, the result of which was the collapse of Fascism, the onset of civil war, and the death of the Duce himself.

2 Diplomacy 1922–32

Italy in 1922 had a secure position in Europe but was unable to exert a great deal of influence, either diplomatically or militarily. The potential threat to her northern frontiers had been removed by the friendship with France and the dismemberment of the Austro-Hungarian Empire, and Italy had no powerful enemies. However, it was Britain and France which were the dominant powers of Europe. They guaranteed the Versailles settlement, their colonies dominated Africa, and their fleets controlled the Mediterranean. Furthermore, France was busy consolidating her political and economic influence in central and eastern Europe, including the Balkans. Any changes in the European *status quo* would require the consent of Britain and France, and, in the absence of a strong Germany to counter-balance them, smaller powers had few means of extracting concessions. A resurgent Italy would have to move carefully. Mussolini was to learn this lesson in his first real foray into European affairs.

* In August 1923 an Italian general and four of his staff were assassinated in Greece. They had been working for the international boundary commission set up under the terms of the peace settlement and were advising on the precise location of the new Greek-Albanian border. On hearing of the assassinations Mussolini blamed the Greek government and demanded a full apology together with 50 million lire in compensation. When the Greeks refused, he ordered the bombardment and occupation of the island of Corfu, off the Greek mainland. The European powers, led by Britain and backed by her Mediterranean fleet, demanded that Italy withdraw. The Duce had little choice but to agree and, although he did receive the 50 million lire compensation, he did not receive a full apology from the Greeks.

The episode was hailed in Italy as a great success for dynamic Fascism, but it also showed that although Mussolini might be able to bully smaller powers, he was unable to stand up to the great powers. This realisation rankled with Mussolini but it made him aware of the necessity of good relations with Britain, at least in the short term. He was fortunate that Austen Chamberlain, Britain's foreign secretary for much of the 1920s, was an admirer of the fledgling Italian regime and was inclined to look tolerantly on the Dictator's actions.

Fascism had more success in the Balkans in 1924 when, in the Pact of Rome, Italy received Fiume, an Italian-speaking town on the Yugoslavian coast. This town had long been a target of Italian territorial ambitions, and had been occupied, if temporarily, by Italian nationalists in 1919 (see page 46). Mussolini's diplomatic success therefore brought him great prestige and popularity.

The Duce's success over Fiume perhaps persuaded him that Yugoslavia could be pushed around. Mussolini resented French influence in Yugoslavia and was keen to demonstrate to this new state, which had only been formed in 1919, that Italy was the dominant power in the region and could make life very difficult for Yugoslavia if it tried to resist Italian influence. An opportunity to illustrate this arose in 1924 when an Italian-sponsored local chieftain, Ahmed Zog, managed to take power in Albania on Yugoslavia's southern border. The Fascist government supplied Zog with money, encouraged Italian companies to invest in the Albanian economy, and employed Italian officers as advisers to the Albanian army. By the time a Treaty of Friendship was signed in 1926 Albania was little more than an Italian satellite. This was clearly a potential military threat to Yugoslavia, a threat emphasised by Mussolini's funding of those ethnic minorities, notably the Croats, who wanted to secede from the Yugoslav state. Yugoslavia responded by doing her best not to antagonise Fascist Italy, but she also refused to be intimidated into subservient status. Throughout the 1930s the Duce maintained his aggressive posture and eventually occupied much of Yugoslavia during the Second World War, after that country's defeat at the hands of Nazi Germany, Italy's ally.

* While the Duce was meddling in the Balkans, he was careful to play the part of a moderate statesman in western Europe, where Britain and France's principal interests lay. Italy remained in the League of Nations – that supposed guarantor of international good conduct – signed the Locarno Treaties, which confirmed the permanence of Germany's western borders, and entered into the Kellogg-Briand Pact of 1928 outlawing war. Italy and Britain also came to agreement over the location of the border between their North African colonial territories, Libya and Egypt. However, Mussolini had little interest in the details of such treaties and pacts and rarely took the time to read them through thoroughly. But he did see the advantages of participating in these diplomatic spectacles. He enjoyed being taken seriously as a European statesman, hoped that his apparent moderation would lead to concessions of some sort from Britain and France, and, perhaps above all, saw an opportunity to enhance his prestige and power at home. He would organise dramatic entrances to international conferences, as when he raced across Lake Maggiore in a flotilla of speedboats to Locarno. Italian press coverage was always extensive, suggesting that the Duce was being treated as an equal by the leaders of the great powers and that Mussolini's presence and contributions had been crucial in reaching such momentous European agreements. This was gross exaggeration – at Locarno, for instance, he attended only one session of the conference and did not even bother to read the final draft of the treaties – but it created a powerful impression in Italy.

* Mussolini was posing as a good neighbour for the eyes of Britain and France, but, by the late 1920s, he was increasingly determined to revise the peace settlement. However, in order to do this he would need friends and stronger armed forces. He signed a friendship treaty in 1927 with Hungary, another revisionist state, and funded right-wing groups

in Germany in the hope that a pro-Fascist government might come to power there. He even went so far as to train German miltary pilots in Italy, a clear breach of Versailles. As for military power, the Dictator told the Italian parliament in 1927 that he would create an airforce 'large enough to blot out the sun', and although he did sign the Kellogg-Briand Pact outlawing war, he immediately dismissed it in a speech to that same parliament. By the early 1930s the Fascist regime was clearly ready to do more than meddle in Balkan affairs and was now prepared to challenge the European *status quo* directly in pursuit of a 'greater' Italy. The 1930s were to see Italy becoming increasingly aggressive not only in the Balkans but in western Europe and Africa too. What had prompted this development?

Historians of the Left have traditionally seen Fascist foreign policy in the 1930s as a means by which the regime attempted to distract public attention away from failures at home, and they suggest that foreign policy became more aggressive and reckless as dissatisfaction intensified within Italy. However, in recent years historians have modified this view: Mussolini certainly did recognise that foreign successes would bolster his regime and that he did perhaps need new, dramatic successes now that domestic policies, such as the Corporate State, were producing disappointing results, but his aims had always been expansionist and aggressive, even if circumstances had caused him to disguise this. Fascist foreign policy became increasingly belligerent partly as the result of frustration with the limited gains won by Italian diplomacy in the 1920s, but mainly due to the recognition that the rise to power of the Nazis had transformed the European situation and opened the way for Italian ambitions.

3 German-Italian relations 1933–5

Mussolini realised in the 1920s that a strong, resurgent Germany, seeking revision of Versailles, would frighten Britain and France and would make them more amenable to Italian demands. Indeed, neither would want Italy as an enemy and she would, therefore, be able to play off the two camps against each other to her own advantage. The dictator had probably funded the Nazis, along with a number of other right-wing groups, in the Germany of the late 1920s. On the face of it, therefore, he should have been delighted about Hitler's accession to power in 1933. But, in fact, early relations between the two regimes were rather difficult.

* Mussolini enjoyed claiming that 'his creation', Fascism, was spreading through Europe, but he was a little apprehensive lest Germany be seen as the centre of Fascism and he be overshadowed by the new Führer. A more concrete concern was that this new German regime might take over Austria, thus creating a powerful 'greater Germany' which would share an Alpine frontier with Italy. If this was

to occur, Italy would have lost the security of her northern border guaranteed by victory over Austria-Hungary in 1918, and might even be pressurised into ceding those German-speaking areas in north-eastern Italy gained at the peace conference.

The danger of an Austro-German union (*Anschluss*) was, of course, even more apparent to the Austrian government in Vienna. Any union of the two countries would not be a merger, it would effectively be the takeover of the weaker (Austria) by the stronger (Germany). Consequently, Dollfuss, the Austrian chancellor, looked for outside support and he visited Rome three times during 1933. He was relieved to be told that he should suppress the Nazi party in Austria and, if the Germans threatened to invade, Austrian independence would be protected by Italian arms.

In February 1934, Mussolini encouraged Dollfuss to set up a right-wing authoritarian regime which would be partly modelled on Italian Fascism, but which would be anti-Nazi. The chancellor attempted to do this but was assassinated by Nazi sympathisers in July 1934. Mussolini was outraged and immediately despatched troops to the Austrian border to deter Germany from attempting an armed *Anschluss*. Relations between the two Fascist regimes had not got off to an auspicious start. Indeed, in 1933 Mussolini had described his fellow dictator as:

> an ideologue who talks more than he governs . . . a muddle-headed fellow; his brain is stuffed with philosophical and political tags that are utterly incoherent.

On hearing of Dollfuss' assassination the Duce went further and called Hitler a 'horrible sexual degenerate'.

* Relations reached a low in March 1935 when Nazi Germany revealed the existence of an air force, the *Luftwaffe*, in breach of Versailles and announced that she was introducing military conscription with a view to creating an army five times the size permitted by the peace treaty. In the face of this challenge, Mussolini agreed to meet the British and French in the Italian town of Stresa to organise a joint response to the apparent German threat. The result was a declaration that the three powers in the 'Stresa Front' would collaborate to prevent any further breaches in the treaties that might threaten peace.

Nevertheless, although Mussolini certainly feared and distrusted Nazi Germany, he realised that Britain and France had just as much, if not more reason, to fear Hitler. A rearmed and hostile Germany reminded the western allies of the horrors of the First World War. The Duce was shrewd enough to make use of this. The 'Stresa Front' gave him added protection against an *Anschluss*, but it also indicated to him that the western powers were anxious to avoid Germany allying with other states to pursue the revision of the peace settlement. Mussolini was convinced that the thought of a German-Italian *rapprochement* would horrify Britain and France. To avoid such a possibility they might be more sympathetic towards Italian ambitions and more tolerant towards Italian adventures overseas. Mussolini saw this an ideal opportunity to expand his colonial empire at minimal risk. His chosen area for expansion was to be Ethiopia.

4 War in Ethiopia

The Duce believed that Italian colonies should be developed and expanded, not for commercial motives such as to secure markets or to extract raw materials, but because the possession of a growing empire would enhance Italy's claim to be a great power. Colonies were also part of Italy's historic destiny. After all, she was the descendant of the Roman Empire which had controlled huge areas of North Africa and had dominated the Mediterranean. The possession of new African territories would provide other benefits. They might be ripe for Italian colonists and would certainly produce large numbers of colonial troops to enhance Italy's military might. Not least, an adventure in Africa offered the prospect of securing military glory on the cheap, impressing the great powers and enhancing the regime's prestige at home.

Ethiopia was an ideal target for Mussolini's ambitions. It was a large country and had not so far been made part of a European country's empire – one of only two African states that had escaped this fate – but it lacked the means to fight a modern war. The neighbouring Italian colonies of Eritrea and Somaliland provided convenient avenues of attack, while the uncertain location of Ethiopia's borders with these colonies might provide 'incidents' between the two countries' armed forces that could be used as a justification for war. Furthermore, a successful conquest would avenge Italy's humiliating defeat by Ethiopia at Adowa in 1896. This, of course, would lend enormous prestige to the Fascist regime at home, proving the Duce's claim that he, and he alone, could restore Italy to international grandeur.

The Fascist government had taken an interest in Ethiopia since the early 1920s and had sought to bring her into an Italian sphere of influence. Italy had sponsored Ethiopia's membership of the League of Nations in 1923 and had even signed a Treaty of Friendship in 1928. Despite these acts of a supposed 'good neighbour', the Fascist regime was, by 1929, drawing up plans to annex the country. In fact, in that year, Italian soldiers did begin to occupy disputed border areas. It was in one of these areas in December 1934 that the incident occurred which gave the Duce an excuse for war. At the oasis of Wal-Wal a skirmish took place between Italian and Ethiopian troops, in which 30 Italian soldiers were killed. Mussolini immediately demanded a full apology and hefty compensation. The Ethiopian government replied by requesting a League of Nations investigation. The League agreed and set up an inquiry.

Mussolini had no interest in waiting for the results of such an investigation, as he had already issued a secret order for the 'total conquest of Ethiopia' in December 1934, and was intent on building up his military forces in the area. A huge army, together with civilian support, totalling half a million men, was transported to Africa. The shock of German rearmament did cause the Duce to pause to consider whether he was leaving himself exposed in Europe, but the Stresa conference assured him that he had nothing to fear. In addition, his conviction that Britain and France were too preoccupied about Germany to oppose him seemed to be confirmed. Talks with their foreign ministers during the first half of 1935 showed that both countries were prepared to accede to Italian control of at least part of Ethiopia. Britain might well object to a full conquest, but her protests would be confined to diplomatic notes.

In October 1935 Italian armies attacked Ethiopia. The previous day the Duce had justified his invasion to the Italian public:

1 It is not only our army that marches to its objective, 44 million Italians march with that army, all united and alert. Let others try to commit the blackest injustice, taking away Italy's place in the sun. When, in 1915, Italy united her fate with the Allies, how
5 many promises were made? To fight the common victory Italy brought her supreme contribution of 670,000 dead, 480,000 disabled and more than one million wounded. When we went to the table of that odious peace they gave us only the crumbs of the colonial booty.

The Ethiopian forces were disorganised and armed with antiquated weapons. They were soon forced on to the defensive and suffered the full effects of modern war. The Italians used aerial bombing and poison gas in their campaigns. In April 1936 the Ethiopian army was heavily defeated at Lake Ashangi and, in the following month, the capital, Addis Ababa, was occupied. The Ethiopian Emperor, Haile Selassie, fled to Britain and organised opposition ceased. However, sporadic guerilla attacks did continue and the Italian forces began a ruthless campaign of suppression which Mussolini was keen to encourage. He sent the following telegrams to his commander in the field:

1 5 June 1936 – All rebels made prisoner are to be shot.
Secret – 8 June 1936. To finish off rebels as at Ancober use gas.
Secret – 8 July 1936. I repeat my authorisation to initiate and systematically conduct policy of terror and extermination against
5 rebels and populations in complicity with them. Without the law of ten eyes for one we cannot heal this wound in good time. Acknowledge.

21 February 1937 – Agreed that male population of Goggetti over
18 years of age is to be shot and village destroyed.

10 21 February 1937 – No persons arrested are to be released
without my order. All civilians and clerics in any way suspect are
to be shot without delay

These brutal tactics did succeed in pacifying Ethiopia, but they did
nothing to reconcile the people to Fascist rule.

  * Nevertheless, the defeat of Ethiopia made the Duce immensely
popular in Italy, although the war had not been quite so popular with
the Italian public at its outset. Some Italians, no doubt, had been taken
in by the orchestrated press campaign stressing Italy's right to an East
African Empire and suggesting the presence of enormous quantities of
valuable resources, and precious metals in Ethiopia, but many remained unenthusiastic. It was the condemnation of the invasion by the
League of Nations that caused the public to rally round the regime in
order to defend the honour of Italy. The League not only protested but

THE MAN WHO TOOK THE LID OFF

The Man Who Took The Lid Off – *cartoon from the* Evening Standard.

also introduced economic sanctions – no arms were to be sold to Italy and member nations were to ban the import of Italian goods. However, these measures were little more than symbolic: there was no ban imposed on the strategic commodities of oil, coal and steel and the Suez Canal was not closed to Italian ships. Had Britain chosen to close this canal, Italy's vital supply route to her forces in East Africa would have been cut off.

These sanctions irritated Mussolini without hindering his war effort. He was convinced that Britain and France, the leading powers in the League, were just 'paper tigers'. His opinion was confirmed by the western powers' reluctance to use the forces at their disposal and by their efforts to bring the conflict to an end by diplomatic means, culminating in the ill-fated Hoare-Laval Pact of December 1935. This agreement between the foreign ministers of Britain and France would have handed over the greater part of Ethiopia to Italy, leaving the Emperor Haile Selassie with only a small, unviable independent state. A public outcry in Britain and France put paid to this agreement, but it appeared to the Duce that the governments of both countries were desperate to avoid having Fascist Italy as an enemy.

Mussolini despised such apparent weakness. He increasingly saw the western democracies as cowardly. The 1933 Oxford University Union debate in which the supposed cream of British youth had argued that they were no longer prepared to 'fight for King and Country' had probably encouraged such a notion. Mussolini thought that Britain and France were decadent, interested only in money making and a comfortable life. His Fascism was, in contrast, dynamic and contemptuous of material comforts. It might even replace 'bourgeois democracy' as the dominant force in Europe.

5 German-Italian Relations 1936–9

Mussolini now looked towards Nazi Germany with more favour – here was another vibrant Fascist regime, one which had played no part in sanctions and which, like Italy, had grievances against Britain and France dating back to the 1919 peace conferences. Italian friendship, with the prospect of a military alliance, with Nazi Germany would terrify Britain and France and would allow the Duce to prise concessions out of them. He was still not sure exactly what these concessions might be, but he could now see the possibility of realising his dream of Mediterranean domination.

* A reconciliation between the two Fascist regimes had begun as early as January 1936 when Hitler agreed not to carry out an *Anschluss* and, in return, Mussolini conceded that Austria would be reduced to the status of a German satellite. Europe became aware of the warming of relations a few months later when Ciano, Italy's foreign minister, visited Berlin, and confirmed the existence of the 'Rome-Berlin Axis'.

This public declaration of friendship was cemented by a secret understanding that Italy would expend her expansionist energies towards the Mediterranean while Germany looked towards eastern Europe and the Baltic, thus ensuring that they did not compete with one another. Hitler even went so far as to suggest that he was preparing his country to be at war in three years time.

Hitler's talk of war did not frighten Mussolini. In fact, he revelled in such bellicose phrases and saw war as the 'supreme test' both of the individual and of the nation. Italy was re-arming and, although he certainly had not committed himself to taking the country into a European war, he was prepared to risk such a conflict in pursuit of his foreign policy goals.

From 1936 the accommodation with Germany was the central fact of Italian foreign policy. German and Italian forces fought on the same side in the Spanish Civil War, supporting the attempts of Spanish conservatives and Fascists to overthrow the elected Republican government. Mussolini had been reluctant to get involved, at first lending only transport planes to the rebels, but when the expected 'Fascist victory' did not materialise the Duce committed Italian troops to avoid a damaging loss of prestige. Eventually, 40,000 Italians were fighting in Spain, being withdrawn only after Republican resistance had collapsed in 1939.

In November 1937 the 'Rome-Berlin Axis' was further strengthened when Italy joined Germany and Japan in the Anti-Comintern Pact. In practice, this was a declaration that the three countries would work together against Soviet Russia. However, the relationship between the two European Fascist states did cool somewhat in March 1938 when Hitler finally carried out the *Anschluss* without consulting the Duce. In response, Mussolini signed an agreement with Britain guaranteeing the *status quo* in the Mediterranean. But the two dictators were soon reconciled. The Duce had no interest in maintaining the *status quo* and, despite his annoyance at not being informed about the *Anschluss*, his admiration for German dynamism only increased.

In September 1938 Hitler's demands over the Sudetenland (an area of Czechoslovakia inhabited mainly by German speakers) seemed likely to lead to a general European war. The British prime minister, Neville Chamberlain, asked Mussolini to act as a mediator at the conference which had been called at Munich to seek a diplomatic solution to the crisis. Mussolini enjoyed the favourable publicity he received in the British and French press, but he was not even-handed as mediator. In fact, he secretly colluded with Hitler to find a compromise favourable to Nazi claims. The Sudetenland was handed over to the Third Reich.

The Duce was hailed in Europe as an architect of peace. But, in his view, Munich had only confirmed the weakness of Britain and France, a weakness on which he was determined to capitalise. In November 1938 the Italian parliament was recalled and Mussolini instructed it to demand the annexation of Nice, Corsica, and Tunis from France. In the same month he told the Grand Council of Fascism,

1 I announce to you the immediate goals of fascist dynamism. As we have avenged Adowa, so will we avenge Valona [an Albanian port abandoned by Italian troops in 1920]. Albania will become Italian. I cannot tell you how or when. But it will come to pass.
5 Then, for the requirements of our security in this Mediterranean that still confines us, we need Tunis and Corsica. The [French] frontier must move to the [river] Var. I do not aim for Savoy, because it is outside the circle of the Alps . . . All this is a programme. I cannot lay down a fixed timetable. I merely
10 indicate the route along which we shall march.

At last Mussolini was beginning to clarify those vague expansionist ideas he had held for well over a decade.

By 1939, with France re-arming and French opinion outraged by Italian territorial claims, the Duce was very aware that if he was to realise his ambitions war was almost inevitable. However, he hoped and believed that he could win a war with France, particularly if he had a military alliance with Germany. As for Britain, he had seen Chamberlain's desperation to avoid war at Munich and believed she would keep out of such a conflict. In February 1939 the Dictator presented his most candid analysis of his foreign policy aims and made it clear that he was even prepared for confrontation with Britain, if need be. He told the Grand Council,

1 States are more or less independent according to their maritime position. In other words, states that possess coasts on the oceans or have free access to the oceans are independent. States that cannot communicate freely with the oceans and are enclosed in
5 inland seas are semi-independent. States that are absolutely continental and have outlets neither on the oceans nor on (inland) seas are not independent.
   Italy belongs to the second category of states. It is bathed by a landlocked sea that communicates with the oceans through the
10 Suez Canal, . . . easily blocked . . . , and through the straits of Gibraltar, dominated by the cannons of Great Britain.
   Italy therefore does not have free connection with the oceans. Italy is therefore in truth a prisoner of the Mediterranean, and the more populous and prosperous Italy becomes, the more its
15 imprisonment will gall.
   The bars of this prison are Corsica, Tunis, Malta, Cyprus. The sentinels of this prison are Gibraltar and Suez. Corsica is a pistol pointed at the heart of Italy; Tunisia at Sicily; while Malta and Cyprus constitute a threat to all our positions in the eastern and

20 western Mediterranean. Greece, Turkey, Egypt have been ready
to form a chain with Great Britain and to complete the politico-
military encirclement of Italy. Greece, Turkey, Egypt must be
considered virtual enemies of Italy and of its expansion. From
this situation . . . one can draw the following conclusions:
25 1. The task of Italian policy, which cannot have and does not
have continental objectives of a territorial nature except Albania,
is to first of all break the bars of the prison.
2. Once the bars are broken, Italy's policy can have only one
watchword – to march to the ocean.
30 Which ocean? The Indian Ocean, joining Libya with Ethiopia
through the Sudan, or the Atlantic, through French North
Africa. In either case, we will find ourselves confronted with
Anglo-French opposition.

That this was not mere bravado was shown by his instructions that
detailed plans be drawn up to invade and formally annex Albania, thus
intimidating Yugoslavia and making the Adriatic virtually an 'Italian
sea'.

While preparations were going ahead for this invasion Mussolini
received a second shock from his German friends. German troops
marched into Czechoslovakia in March 1939. Again, as over the
Anschluss, he was furious and again contemplated changing sides. Such
thoughts of a major switch in policy lasted no longer than similar ideas a
year earlier. Real fear of Germany was now added to grudging
admiration for her successes. The Nazi state seemed intent on redraw-
ing the map of Europe and Mussolini was convinced it had the military
resources to achieve this even against the combined armies of Britain
and France. Surely it was better to be friends with such a dynamic
regime and pick up some of the spoils of victory?

The Italian invasion of Albania finally took place in April 1939 and
put the Duce back in the limelight. Fascist Italy was also realising her
destiny by taking over weaker and 'inferior' states. The Italian regime
conveniently ignored the fact that Albania had been a satellite for over
ten years. Victory was won without any major fighting.

If Mussolini was delighted with his success, he was angry that his
Albanian adventure had caused Britain and France to give guarantees of
military assistance to Greece and Turkey should they too be attacked.
To the Duce these guarantees were an aggressive move against
legitimate Italian interests: Mussolini had long considered Greece as
within Italy's sphere of influence and he had been trying to emphasise
this point in 1923 when he had bombarded Corfu.

★ These guarantees may have finally convinced Mussolini to conclude
a military alliance with Germany, but, in any case, such an alliance was
the logical conclusion of Italian actions since Ethiopia. The 'Pact of
Steel' was signed in May 1939. It committed both nations to join the

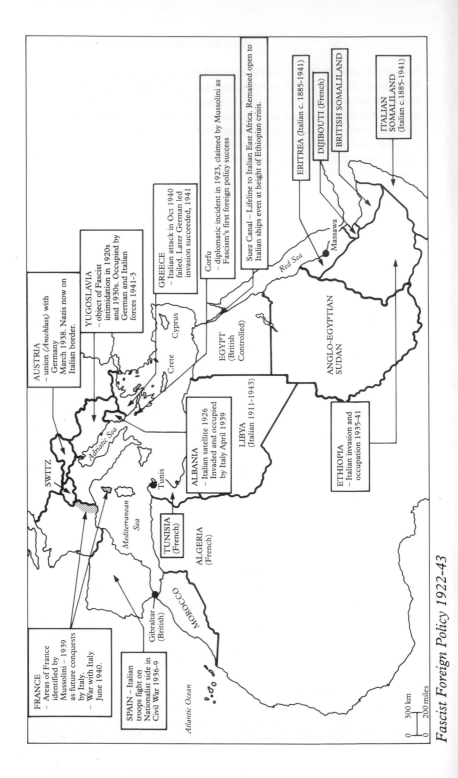

FRANCE
– Areas of France identified by Mussolini – 1939 as future conquests by Italy.
– War with Italy June 1940.

SPAIN – Italian troops fight on Nationalist side in Civil War 1936-9

Gibraltar (British)

MOROCCO

Atlantic Ocean

ALGERIA (French)

TUNISIA (French)

Tunis

Mediterranean Sea

SWITZ

Adriatic Sea

AUSTRIA
– union (Anschluss) with Germany March 1938. Nazis now on Italian border.

YUGOSLAVIA
– object of Fascist intimidation in 1920s and 1930s. Occupied by German and Italian forces 1941-3

ALBANIA
– Italian satellite 1926 Invaded and occupied by Italy April 1939

LIBYA
(Italian 1911-1943)

Crete

Cyprus

GREECE
– Italian attack in Oct 1940 failed. Later German led invasion succeeded, 1941

Corfu
– diplomatic incident in 1923, claimed by Mussolini as Fascism's first foreign policy success

EGYPT
(British Controlled)

Suez Canal – Lifeline to Italian East Africa. Remained open to Italian ships even at height of Ethiopian crisis.

Red Sea

Massawa

ERITREA (Italian c. 1885-1941)

DJIBOUTI (French)

BRITISH SOMALILAND

ITALIAN SOMALILAND (Italian c.1885-1941)

ANGLO-EGYPTIAN SUDAN

ETHIOPIA
– Italian invasion and occupation 1935-41

0   300 km
0   200 miles

Fascist Foreign Policy 1922-43

other in war even if that other country had caused the war by an act of aggression. In short, if Germany were to provoke a war with Britain and France, Italy would be duty bound to enter the war on Germany's side. It is uncertain why Mussolini agreed to such terms. Indeed, it has been suggested that he took no notice of the precise wording of treaties, regarding them as simply pieces of paper which could be discarded whenever it suited him to do so. Whether or not Mussolini understood the full consequences of the agreement when he signed it, his government soon realised its meaning and took fright. Ciano, the foreign secretary, seems to have persuaded his Duce that Italy should make its position clear to her German ally. Consequently, at the end of May the Fascist government told the Germans that, although there was no doubt about Italy's willingness to go to war, any war should be postponed for at least three years to allow her to rearm fully. Hitler ignored this appeal, not even bothering to reply.

The Duce did not press the point, perhaps because it made him appear foolish and cowardly, and he made no attempt to delay Hitler's preparations for the invasion of Poland. Only at the end of August, when the attack was imminent, did he repeat his assertion that Italy needed several more years of peace. Hitler again ignored this and demanded that Italy stand by the terms of the 'Pact of Steel'. Mussolini realised that Italy was not yet in a position to fight, that such a war would be unpopular in Italy, and that the war would not be fought for Italian interests. He therefore attempted to wriggle out of his obligations by arguing that Italy would join the war only if she was supplied with enormous, and unrealistic, quantities of war materiel. When Germany and the western democracies went to war over Poland in September, the Duce declared that his ally had been 'treacherous' and had thereby made the Pact defunct. It was then announced that Italy would be a ' non-belligerent'. The overwhelming majority of Italians were greatly relieved.

6 Non-belligerence, September 1939–June 1940

Mussolini hated Italy's neutrality. It made him look rather pathetic after all his bellicose talk. However, he realised that the risks of intervention, both for his country and consequently for his regime, were too great. Throughout the winter of 1939 the supposedly dynamic, decisive Duce could not make up his mind what policy to pursue. He still favoured Germany, but could be jealous of Nazi successes and, at one point, even considered acting as a mediator to bring the sides to the negotiating table.

On 10 May 1940 Hitler launched his *Blitzkrieg* against France and the Low Countries, catching the Allied forces by surprise and throwing them into disarray. Holland surrendered within five days and within another week the German armies had reached the Channel coast.

Belgium surrendered and, by the end of May, the British Expeditionary Force had left the continent after a desperate evacuation from Dunkirk. German forces were sweeping through France and were meeting only disorganised opposition.

It appeared to Mussolini, and indeed to the watching world, that the western allies were on the brink of total defeat. France would almost certainly collapse within days and Britain, left to fight the war alone, would probably follow within a few months or else seek a humiliating negotiated peace. The view from Rome was that if Italy remained neutral she would be faced with a Europe dominated by Germany, a Germany angry at Italy's refusal to honour her treaty obligations. Italy would have gained nothing, would be in even less position to assert great power status, and be herself under physical threat from her Nazi neighbour. On the other hand, if Italy now committed herself to the Axis cause, Germany would be a friend and not a potential enemy. Italy and Germany would share Europe, with the Italians possibly having a free hand in the Mediterranean. In June 1940 Mussolini, therefore, decided to seize what he thought was the opportunity to redeem his lost honour and to win military glory. He declared war on Britain and France.

7 Italy in the Second World War

Within a week of Italy's entry into war France surrendered to the Germans. Mussolini was more than ever convinced that Britain would soon follow, and he was determined to seize as much territory as possible before any peace settlement. Consequently, in September 1940, he ordered his forces in Libya to attack British positions in Egypt and, in the following month, he launched the Italian army in Albania against Greece. However, both offensives rapidly ground to a halt and by the end of the year the Fascist armies had been pushed back into Libya and Albania respectively. The navy fared no better, losing half its battle fleet to a British air attack on the port of Taranto in November.

Hopes of military glory on the cheap were now fading. Britain still controlled Egypt and most of the Mediterranean and had thwarted German plans to invade across the English Channel. The Duce, nevertheless, remained confident of ultimate victory. However, his Fascist ally lacked faith in Italian arms. In February 1941 Mussolini was persuaded, reluctantly, to accept the German General Rommel as Axis commander in North Africa. In April German armies finally ended the stalemate in the Balkans, sweeping through Yugoslavia and defeating Greece in little more than a week. The Axis powers appeared to be winning, but it was becoming increasingly clear that Italy was not just a junior partner to Germany but was also a subservient one. Italy relied on Germany for raw materials, particularly coal, and found that the crucial political and military decisions were taken by the Germans, usually without any consultation. Mussolini resented this dependency but could do little about it. The loss of Italy's East African empire to British troops in April 1941 was final proof of her military failure. The Duce did manage to send 200,000 soldiers to the Russian front, but these men were too poorly trained and equipped to be of real value. If Italy was to gain anything at all from the war it would be through German success not her own, while German defeat would bring down Italian Fascism with it.

In 1942 there were some modest Axis successes in Russia and North Africa, but by the end of the year the Germans were on the brink of catastrophic defeat at Stalingrad and Rommel's forces in North Africa were in full retreat. Libya was abandoned to the British in January 1943 and by May the whole Axis army in North Africa had surrendered. Two months later the Anglo-American forces landed in Sicily. The invasion of the Italian mainland itself was imminent.

8 The Fall of Mussolini

Public opinion had been divided over the decision to enter the war in June 1940. There had been many doubters, but a significant number of Italians had hoped for a quick and profitable victory. Defeats in Greece and Egypt had soon destroyed such optimism. Those Italians who had believed the Fascist propaganda about an army of eight million bayonets and an air force that could 'blot out the sun' became particularly disillusioned when they witnessed the organisational chaos, the antiquated weaponry and the paucity of battle training. Soldiers home on leave could recount how the attack on Greece had begun at the start of the rainy season and how, once winter set in, the army could provide only totally inadequate winter clothing. Veterans of the North African campaign could describe the desperate shortage of armoured vehicles.

Italian civilians, in any case, did not need to be told about Fascism's lack of preparedness for a prolonged war – they could see the evidence all around them. The regime's conviction that the war would be brief meant that no plans had been drawn up to mobilise the economy for full-scale war production. Food became short as grain imports fell – the result of British naval blockade in the Mediterranean – and, since the government refused to introduce rationing, prices rose dramatically. Coffee, petrol and soap became virtually unobtainable, except for those rich enough to afford the prices on the flourishing black market. Eventually, in 1941, rationing was introduced, but by then stocks had run very low. Supplies were scarce and badly organised and ordinary Italians were faced with a bread ration of only 150 grams per person per day – the lowest of any combatant country except the USSR.

By the end of 1940 the Italian public was heartily sick of the war. Their faith in the Duce's infallibility had been shattered. There was no longer any interest in the possible spoils of war, particularly as it was becoming increasingly apparent that further fighting would only increase German control over the country. The years 1941 and 1942 only increased the disillusionment of the Italian public, as defeat followed defeat, as shortages worsened, and as working hours lengthened. Opposition groups, from communist to catholic, began to emerge. These groups were still small and disorganised, but, in early 1943, shortages and anti-war sentiment did lead to a wave of strikes in Italian industry.

The regime was well aware of the deep unpopularity of the war and the growing contempt for the Duce. By late 1942 prominent Fascists, notably Ciano, the Dictator's own son-in-law, were inclined to make peace. Their realisation that Mussolini would not contemplate this, and that the Allies would not negotiate with him anyway, led them to the belief that the Duce must go. He could be a sacrifice or a scapegoat, peace could be arranged, and the Fascists might keep at least some of their power. Such views were echoed at the court of King Victor Emmanuel, and among the leading generals, who feared a collapse of social order.

The Allied conquest of Sicily in July 1943 was the final straw – the mainland was in danger of invasion and utter defeat appeared inevitable. A group of senior Fascists led by Roberto Farinacci, the ex-squad leader, and De Bono, a Fascist general in the Ethiopian campaign, persuaded Mussolini to call a meeting of the Grand Council of Fascism to discuss the military situation. The Grand Council, which had not sat since 1939, met on the night of 24–25 July 1943 and voted 19–7 to ask the king to restore all those powers to parliament, ministers and Grand Council that Mussolini had taken away. In effect, they were seeking a way to get rid of the Duce, make peace, and save, if not the regime, then at least themselves.

The members of the Grand Council had expected a spirited defence, and even physical violence, from Mussolini and they were surprised to see the Dictator subdued, perhaps ill. He could not bring himself to protest. But by the morning of 25 July the Duce had recovered himself and he visited the king, intending to name new ministers, punish those who had voted against him, and continue the war. However, the king, encouraged by the events of the previous night and spurred on by the army high command, declared that the war was lost and that Marshal Badoglio would take over as prime minister with a brief to make peace. The Duce was then arrested.

With the dismissal of Mussolini, the Fascist regime collapsed. There were no public protests, only public relief. Fascists, far from attempting to restore the Duce by calling supporters into the streets, meekly accepted the change in government. Leading Fascists tried to ingratiate themselves with the new prime minister. Even the Fascist mouthpiece, the *Popolo d'Italia*, simply replaced Mussolini's photograph on the front page with that of Marshal Badoglio. It had been a bloodless *coup*. Badoglio arranged an armistice with Britain and the USA in September 1943, but it was Italy's misfortune that this did not bring peace. Nazi Germany could not afford to let this 'backdoor' to Europe fall into Allied hands and promptly occupied northern and central Italy. The Germans then rescued the fallen Dictator from his luxury prison in the Apennine mountains. The Duce was to see out his last two years as the puppet ruler of a German dominated northern Italy. His only consolation was that he could now attempt to wreak vengeance on those Grand Council members who had voted against him. Ciano and De Bono were promptly shot, but the others escaped by going into hiding.

As the Allied forces pushed slowly northwards during 1944 and early 1945, northern Italy degenerated into civil war. Resistance groups sprung up, attacking German soldiers and remaining Italian Fascists. In response, Fascist gangs re-emerged, backed by German arms. These gangs owed little allegiance to the Duce. For the most part they were concerned with making the most of the chaos, organising protection rackets and intimidating civilians for financial gain.

At the beginning of 1945 the Nazi forces were in full retreat towards the Austrian border. Mussolini, surrounded by a dwindling band of supporters, tried to flee. On 25 April he joined a group of German soldiers heading for Austria and disguised himself in a German uniform. At Dongo on Lake Garda the group was stopped by Italian communist partisans. The Duce was recognised. He and his mistress, Clara Petacci, were executed by the partisans on 28 April. Their bodies were taken to Milan and put on public display, strung up by the heels from a garage roof.

9 Assessment

Why were Mussolini's hopes of international greatness for Italy eventually dashed?

Mussolini's foreign policy goals were far too ambitious. It was wholly unrealistic to imagine an Italy simultaneously dominating the Mediterranean miltarily, expanding her colonial empire, and exercising economic and even political control over the Balkans. To have achieved even one of these aims Italy would have required far-sighted leadership, efficient and modernised armed forces, a committed populace, and, above all, an advanced industrialised economy geared for war. The Fascist state possessed none of these assets.

The events of the 1920s and early 1930s had proved that Italy was not strong enough to prise major concessions from Britain and France by diplomatic means. Italy had established political control over Albania, appeared to be Austria's protector against a German-imposed *Anschluss*, and had played a highly-publicised part in international conferences, but this was far from being 'great, respected, and feared'. Certainly,

Hitler's rise to power did make Britain and France more tolerant towards Italian ambitions, but Mussolini was unable to adopt the role of the 'balancing power', able to exact concessions from both sides. The western democracies would have preferred Mussolini as an ally or, more probably, as a moderating influence on the Nazi Dictator, but Fascist Italy's aggressive behaviour in Ethiopia and the Spanish Civil War seemed to indicate that the Duce had little interest in keeping the peace. The western powers continued to deal with Mussolini, hoping that he might restrain his Nazi friend, but by the end of 1938 they had learned to expect very little from him. It was clear to them that he was temperamentally disposed towards Germany and that whatever his territorial demands were, they were impossible to concede. As for Germany, Hitler preferred Italy as an ally but did not take her seriously as a military power. Italian neutrality or hostility would not have deflected the Führer from his foreign policy goals. Indeed, both the *Anschluss* and the seizure of Czechoslovakia showed an insensitivity towards Italian interests, and when Germany did go to war against Britain and France in September 1939 the Nazis were neither surprised nor concerned by Mussolini's 'non-belligerence'.

Diplomatic methods had not succeeded in realising the Duce's ambitions and the events of 1940–3 were to prove that could war not lead to the permanent expansion of the Fascist state. In fact, it would cause its destruction. Admittedly, in June 1940 Italy did appear to be in an advantageous position with France on the brink of defeat and Britain severely weakened. Italy's armed forces were however ill-prepared for a major war. Large sums had been spent on rearmament – in the period 1935–8 Italy spent 11.8 per cent of her national income on her armed forces, compared to 12.9 per cent in Germany, 6.9 per cent in France, and 5.5 per cent in Britain – but much of this money had been squandered on purchasing inadequate weaponry and on providing luxurious living quarters for officers. The Italian armed forces were also to prove themselves inefficient and incompetent.

The navy, probably the best-equipped of the three services, was reluctant to risk its new battleships against a vulnerable British Mediterranean fleet and adopted a defensive strategy throughout the war. As for the submarine branch, its numerical superiority over the British was offset by technical inferiority, and one third of Italy's submarines were sunk in the first three weeks of the war.

The air force possessed only 1,000 effective planes with which to 'blot out the sun' and these were also of inferior quality. For example, the main fighter aircraft, the Fiat CR42 biplane, was slow, under-armed, and was grounded in large numbers during the North African campaigns for want of sand filters for the engines.

The army was even more outdated. Mussolini claimed he had 'eight million bayonets' ready for service, but in June 1940 less than 0.8 million men were ready to fight and these were largely equipped with rifles and artillery dating back to the First World War. Above all, the Italian army was lacking in tanks. The Second World War was to be a mechanised war but, in 1940, Italy possessed only about 1,500 armoured cars and light tanks.

The Italian soldier was not only poorly-equipped, he was also poorly trained and badly led. The generals, of whom there were over 600, were steeped in the defensive traditions of the First World War and were sceptical of armoured warfare and air support. It was largely Mussolini's fault that the generals were incompetent. He concentrated power in his own hands, promoting officers more for their obedience and powers of flattery than for their military expertise.

The war effort was hindered further by the fact that the Italian economy was still poorly prepared for sustained, large-scale armaments production. Strategic materials, notably coal and iron ore, had to be imported from Germany and German-occupied territories. As the war began to go badly for the Axis, the Germans were increasingly reluctant to divert such scarce resources to their ineffectual Italian allies. This, together with the absence of long-term planning, led to a fall of 20 per cent in Italian steel production between 1940 and 1942 with the result that losses, particularly in tanks and aircraft, could not be replaced. Food production also fell. The wheat harvest dropped by 1.5 million tonnes as a result of many peasant farmers being drafted into the army. Autarky had certainly not been achieved.

Food shortages, government inefficiency, and military defeats destroyed the confidence of a population which had never been truly committed to Italian expansionism. By the end of 1940, just six months after Italy's entry into the war, the chief of military intelligence could report that 'most people want the war to end, at whatever cost'. Such attitudes increasingly pervaded the workplace and the armed forces themselves, making the chances of victory even more remote.

Mussolini's war was his attempt to realise his idea of Italian greatness by taking advantage of Hitler's apparent victory in 1940. But the Duce completely misjudged the eventual course of the war. Yet, even an Axis victory would not have given him the power and status he craved. Fascist Italy would have been a relatively modest power in a Europe wholly dominated by Nazi Germany.

Making notes on 'Mussolini and the Wider World'

Questions on foreign policy usually revolve around (i) Mussolini's aims, (ii) the extent to which he realised these aims, and (iii) the reasons for his ultimate failure. It is unlikely that you will need detailed factual knowledge about individual episodes in foreign policy (e.g. the Stresa

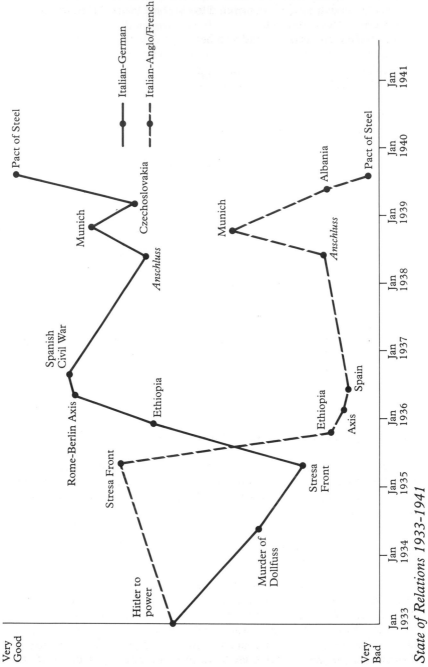

State of Relations 1933–1941

Front) so only make brief notes about such events. However, do think about how each episode is connected to the three issues listed in the first sentence of this paragraph.

The following headings and sub-headings should help you:

1. Aims.
2. Diplomacy 1922–32 (the situation in 1922).
2.1 Policy towards Balkans (Corfu, Yugoslavia, Albania).
2.2 Policy in Western Europe (Locarno, Kellogg-Briand).
2.3 Revisionism.
3. German-Italian relations 1933–5 (attitude towards Germany's growing strength).
3.1 Barriers to friendship (motives for policy over Austria).
3.2 Stresa Front (Italian motives).
4. War in Ethiopia (motives).
4.1 Consequences (Italian public opinion, hostility of Britain and France).
5. German-Italian relations 1936–9 (effect of Ethiopian war).
5.1 Improved relations (Rome-Berlin Axis, Spain, Munich).
5.2 Pact of Steel.
6. Non-belligerence (motives).
7. Italy in the Second World War (reasons for involvement, military defeats).
8. Fall of Mussolini (reasons, consequences for Italy).
9. Assessment. (Why were Mussolini's hopes of international greatness dashed?)

Answering essay questions on 'Mussolini and the Wider World'

There are two basic types of questions on this topic. The first type deals solely with foreign policy and the second (more common) type requires the student to examine foreign policy in the wider context of Mussolini's regime.

Essay questions limited to foreign policy are usually variants of:

1. How successful was Mussolini in realising his foreign policy goals by the end of 1940?

It is important not to ignore the date specified in such a question and to avoid writing a narrative account of 'what Mussolini did' until his downfall in 1943. Such an answer would not score many marks! The question clearly demands an analytical approach of Mussolini's policy up to 1940. One way to prepare for this is to make a list of events in Fascist foreign policy and then to re-read the opening section of the chapter on 'Aims'. Try to match as many events as possible to these 'Aims' and add just one or two sentences explaining how each event matches up. Add another sentence saying whether, or to what extent, the event helped to achieve his aim. Now re-read your notes and decide your answer to the question posed in the essay title. Your answer will be either 'He was generally successful . . .' or 'He was generally unsuccessful . . .', or 'He was successful in these ways . . . but not in these . . .'. This should be the main point of your opening paragraph. The rest of your essay will attempt to justify and explain your answer.

Questions requiring knowledge of the regime as a whole include:

2. To what extent did the Duce's regime give Italians grounds for satisfaction in the period 1922–40?

Here you will need to remember that not all Italians would agree. For example, was Ethiopia a glorious victory or an expensive attack on a generally worthless piece of territory?

Even such questions as:

3. 'Fascism in Italy relied on publicity and propaganda rather than on solid achievement.' Discuss. and,
4. To what extent was the Duce consistent in his beliefs?

demand some discussion of foreign policy. The first question would enable you to point out such things as the discrepancy between Mussolini's claims to possess 'eight million bayonets' and the reality of an ineffective army. The second question should include a discussion of whether he was consistent in his foreign policy goals and the extent to which these were consistent with his domestic policies.

Source-based questions on 'Mussolini and the Wider World'

1 War in Ethiopia
Carefully read Mussolini's speech and his telegrams on pages 122 and 123, and examine the cartoon on page 123. Answer the following questions:

  a) Which 'odious peace' does Mussolini refer to in his speech and why does he describe it as 'odious'? (*3 marks*)
  b) What was the purpose of his speech? (*2 marks*)
  c) What is the cartoonist's attitude towards Mussolini's actions in Ethiopia? Explain your answer. (*3 marks*)
  d) Do you think the cartoonist was exaggerating the possible consequences of the Ethiopian War? Explain your answer. (*3 marks*)
  e) What do the telegrams reveal about the problems Italy faced in Ethiopia during and after 1936? (*4 marks*)
  f) Using the speech and the telegrams, explain Mussolini's attitude towards colonial possessions. (*5 marks*)

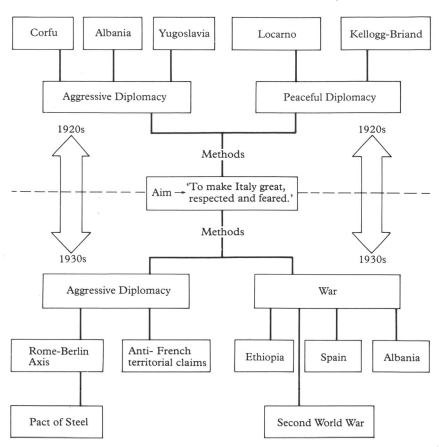

Summary – Mussolini and the Wider World

2 Foreign Policy Goals 1938–9

Carefully read the speeches delivered by Mussolini in November 1938 and February 1939 (pages 126 and 127) and examine the map on page 128. Answer the following questions:

a) What did Mussolini mean, in his November speech, by 'as we have avenged Adowa'? (*2 marks*)

b) Explain what Mussolini meant, in his February speech, by describing Italy as a 'prisoner of the Mediterranean'? (*2 marks*)

c) Using evidence from the speeches, describe the changes in policy that had taken place between November 1938 and February 1939. (*5 marks*)

d) Using the speeches and the map, explain why Italian policy was likely to bring it into conflict with Britain and France. (*7 marks*)

e) How convincing do you find Mussolini's argument about Italy's 'imprisonment'? Explain your answer. (*4 marks*)

CHAPTER 8

Italy since 1945: Continuity and Change

The civil war resulting from the German occupation of northern Italy in 1943 and their installation of a puppet regime under the ailing Duce pitted Italian against Italian. The presence of informants and the brutal reprisals following partisan attacks created an atmosphere of fear and suspicion. Hunger and runaway inflation, together with frustration at the painfully slow advance of the Allied armies, only increased the misery of ordinary Italians.

The anti-Fascist struggle did, however, have some positive consequences. The bravery and determination of the Italian resistance impressed upon the Allies the fact that the inhabitants of Mussolini's Italy were just as much the victims of Fascism as were those peoples, from Ethiopia to Greece, who had been attacked by the Duce's forces. The Partisans' efforts helped convince the Allies that Italy did not deserve to be harshly treated in the peace settlement.

Of equal importance was the rejuvenation of the old parties of Liberal Italy, the *Popolari*, now known as the Christian Democrats, and the Communists, in particular.

Encouraged by the Pope, the various catholic lay groups, never wholly repressed by the Fascists, reformed their political organisation in 1943 and played a prominent role in the partisan movement. The Communists had not taken mass support away from the Socialists during the Liberal period and they had been of limited political significance, but the experience of war had transformed their fortunes. They had retained a small, skeleton organisation throughout the 1930s, and from 1943 their membership increased to two million as workers, inspired by the exploits of the Soviet Red Army, joined the anti-Fascist resistance. For the first time the catholics and the left co-operated, working together in the Committees of National Liberation which took over the administration of the northern cities in April 1945.

In this atmosphere of co-operation it appeared that the new Italian state, when it emerged, would be acceptable to nearly all shades of political opinion within the country. Unlike its Liberal predecessor, the new regime would not be viewed with suspicion and hostility by large sections of Italian society. In fact, many Italians felt that the experience of the resistance opened the way to a second, more perfect *Risorgimento* which would finally unite the whole Italian nation.

As the war ended, this optimism seemed quite justified. The remains of the Fascist state withered away and, although there were some revenge killings and executions, notably of Mussolini, and the ex-party secretaries Starace and Farinacci, there was no bloodbath. The first free government of Italy since 1922 was set up in June 1945 under the leadership of a resistance hero, Ferruccio Parri. However, Parri's Action Party proved too small to dominate the governing coalition and, in November, he was replaced as prime minister by Alcide De Gasperi of the Christian Democrats. De Gasperi's coalition continued to include both the Socialists and the Communists.

Elections for a Constituent Assembly which would draw up a new constitution were called for June 1946. For the first time Italian women would be allowed to vote. In these elections the Christian Democrats won 35 per cent of the vote, with the Socialists and Communists taking 21 per cent and 19 per cent respectively. The remains of the old Liberal party could only secure 7 per cent of the votes cast. It was quite apparent that the Christian Democrats had displaced them as the party of the centre-right and could command the support not only of catholics but also of businessmen and the urban middle classes.

The spirit of co-operation survived the election campaign and the governing coalition held together. A new constitution was drawn up, establishing an Italian democracy and confirming the relationship between Church and state set out in Mussolini's Lateran Accords of 1929. However, there was to be no place for the monarchy. A referendum on the future of the monarchy had been held at the same time as the elections for the Constituent Assembly and 54 per cent of Italians had voted for a republic. The members of the royal family – the House of Savoy (which had never been much loved) – left the country immediately.

By the beginning of 1948 the future seemed bright. The new constitution was ready to be introduced and all the major parties were committed to the idea of an Italian parliamentary democracy. Support for the far right had dissolved, while on the left the Communists and Socialists had dropped their old ideas of revolution and the expropriation of private land and industry. In the economic sphere, the government had curbed inflation and production had been restored to pre-war levels. With $2 billion of American aid in the offing rapid economic recovery seemed assured. Italy had also emerged from the peace settlement relatively unscathed. She had lost her colonial empire, but relatively few Italians had ever been inspired by the notion of empire. Istria and the city of Fiume were handed over to Yugoslavia but Italy was allowed to remain territorially intact. $360 million was demanded as reparations for damage done to Yugoslavia, Albania, Greece, Ethiopia and even Russia, but Italy was relieved that Britain and the USA did not press their own claims.

Italy, then, appeared to have been freed from many of its old problems: there should no longer be those suspicions and bitter political divisions which had plagued the liberal regime, particularly in the early 1920s. The antagonism between catholics and an anti-clerical state would be a thing of the past, and the desire for foreign adventure and national glory would have lost its dangerous appeal. Italy would now become a genuine and successful democracy with all its citizens sharing in the fruits of economic growth.

Despite the fact that most Italians shared such sentiments, there has been little agreement in the years since 1948 over whether the new Italy has managed to live up to these hopes and aspirations. To critics, principally but not exclusively on the left, Italy has not become a genuine democracy and too many of the old problems remain unsolved. They point out that the spirit of party co-operation ended rather abruptly in 1948 when the Christian Democrats expelled the Socialists and Communists from the governing coalition. Since then the Christian Democrats have been the principal partner in every government. This continuous exposure to power, critics argue, has led to political corruption. Christian Democrat dominated governments have expanded the public sector of the economy and jobs and contracts have been handed to their political supporters. In the south, state funds have been directed not towards the areas of greatest need, but have instead been given to projects which would benefit the careers of local Christian Democrat politicians. This seems all too reminiscent of the old liberal regime and its clientage system.

Critics also claim that the electoral system has led to weak coalition governments. Under a voting system of proportional representation no single party has been able to secure a parliamentary majority and consequently coalition governments have been the norm. That the largest single party, the Christian Democrats, has so many factions within it only complicates matters further. With so many different groups able to withdraw their support and bring down the government, it is not surprising that prime ministers have been reluctant to tackle large controversial issues. As it is, in the period 1945–89 there were over 40 Italian governments with the composition of each one determined not so much by the voters but by politicians 'horse-trading in smoke filled rooms'. Similar criticisms were, of course, also directed against the politicians of the liberal regime.

Government unwillingness or inability to address major problems has once again been to the detriment of the south. Northern industry has always taken priority over southern agriculture, while the new industry which has been established in the south has employed relatively few people. Poverty has remained a depressing fact of life. In 1951 income per head in the south was only 63 per cent of the national average, by 1961 it had actually fallen to 62 per cent, and by the end of the 1980s the gap had closed only slightly. Emigration overseas and migration to the northern cities has continued, with 2.5 million southerners travelling north during the 1950s and 1960s. Poverty has contributed to a rise in crime, particularly organised crime. The Sicilian and Calabrian Mafia and the Camorra, their counterparts in Naples, have dramatically expanded their activities to take advantage of the European and North

American drugs trades. Murders of policemen and judges became increasingly frequent during the 1980s.

Given their economic problems it is hardly surprising, critics allege, that southerners have little more sense of Italian identity than did their great-grandparents in the last quarter of the nineteenth century. The example of the 1990 soccer World Cup, held in Italy, has been used to illustrate the point. Before the semi-final in Naples, between Italy and Argentina, the captain of Argentina and star of the local Naples side, Diego Maradona, appealed to the crowd to support his team arguing that they, as southerners, were either ignored or treated with contempt by northern Italians. To the dismay of the Italian press, a section of the crowd actually supported Argentina.

Scandals involving leading politicians and evidence of political alienation among Italians have been taken as final proof of the failure of the Italian state. The most notorious scandal was revealed in 1981 and involved up to 900 prominent politicians, judges, businessmen, and generals. These men were allegedly members of a secret freemasons' lodge, known as P2, and used their contacts in the police and the secret service to collect information with which to blackmail other politicians. The *Banco Ambrosiano* financial scandal, also in the early 1980s, implicated leading bankers and politicians. Surveys have suggested that such episodes have only confirmed the quite widespread belief that politics and politicians are corrupt. Once again, critics have seen a parallel with the Liberal regime whose politicians were also suspected of financial misdemeanours.

The most extreme example of such political alienation has been a terrorist group known as the Red Brigades. This small, far-left group believed parliamentary democracy to be a sham and hoped to pave the way for the overthrow of the state. For a time, in the 1970s and early 1980s, their attacks on leading politicians, policemen, and businessmen dominated the news.

Supporters of the Italian regime, in contrast, see the Red Brigades as a tiny unrepresentative minority of no political significance and contend that the achievements of the state since 1945 have been impressive. They argue that the vast majority of Italians have shown their basic confidence in the regime by continuing to vote in very large numbers for those parties which uphold the political system. Support for extremist parties on both left and right has been negligible. The Christian Democrats have dominated government but only because they have represented such a broad body of opinion, principally on the centre-right. This was something the old Liberalism had never been able to achieve and which had contributed to its downfall.

Furthermore, the dominance of the Christian Democrats has not deprived the Socialists and Communists of all power and influence. Since 1962 the Socialists have quite often been part of the governing coalition and even provided one of the longer serving prime ministers,

Bettino Craxi. The Communists have enjoyed success in local government, controlling a number of sizeable towns and cities. Crucially, both
Communists and Socialists have been willing to work through parliament, an approach which they had rejected in the early 1920s and
which had helped the Fascists come to power.

As for the allegation that governments have changed far too frequently, apologists for the regime argue that, although the prime minister
might change when a government falls, most ministers keep their posts
and ensure continuity in policy. Nor have governments been too weak
or unwilling to adopt bold policies or to address difficult issues. Even
that most intractable of problems, the south, has been tackled and with
some real success. Improved water supplies and better health facilities
have increased life expectancy among southerners. Peasants were the
beneficiaries when the large landed estates were broken up after 1950,
while all southerners gained from the public works schemes designed to
improve the infrastructure and establish new industries. The Liberals
in the early years of the century had considered such an approach and
made some progress in the south, but never on the scale achieved after
1950. The result of these efforts has been the tripling of the average
southerner's income in the 25 years after 1945.

This economic progress has certainly not been confined to the south.
Italians began to enjoy a standard of living only dreamt of by previous
generations. In fact, such was the economic growth after 1950 that
living standards for the average Italian were on a par with those in
Britain by the end of the 1980s. Indeed, GNP was set to surpass that of
Britain – the country which had been the 'workshop of the world' when
Cavour and Garibaldi were still bringing about the unification of the
Italian peninsula.

In the wider world Italy has long given up her taste for aggressive
foreign adventures in pursuit of great power status. She has committed
herself to co-operation with the other western democracies, joining
NATO and being a founder member of the EEC. Italian foreign policy
does not pursue national glory. Instead, it promotes greater European
political and economic unity.

Supporters of the modern Italian state would argue that the words
used by G.M.Trevelyan to descibe Italy in the years before 1914 are
more appropriate to the Italy of the 1990s – 'Nothing is more
remarkable than the stability of the Italian (state) . . . and the building
is as safe as any in Europe. The foundations of human liberty and the
foundations of social order exist there on a firm basis.'

Making notes on 'Italy since 1945: Continuity and Change'

This chapter does not attempt to provide a comprehensive account of Italian history since 1945. That would be beyond the scope of this book. The chapter is intended to stimulate the reader into further thought on the questions central to the whole book – 'What were the problems faced by the Liberal regime between 1870 and 1914 and how successful were the Liberals in solving these problems?', 'Why did the Liberal regime collapse?', and 'Why did Fascism rise to power and what did it achieve?'

You will probably only need to make very brief notes on this chapter. The following questions should help you to organise your thinking, although you may need to look at your notes on chapters 2, 3, and 4 again before you write anything.

1. What does the anti-Fascist resistance and the the disappearance of the Fascist state suggest about the nature and depth of Fascist support?
2. Why have the Christian Democrats been able to secure such support at the polls since 1945? Why did no party manage to win the support of so many people on the centre-right in the years before 1922?
3. How have the parties of the left changed their attitude towards the Italian state since 1945? How important was the left in bringing the Fascists to power?
4. What criticisms have been made of the modern Italian state? Are there any parallels with the Liberal regime pre-1922? If there are parallels, does this affect our analysis of the achievements, failures, and weaknesses of the Liberal regime?
5. How have supporters defended the modern Italian state? Are there any parallels with the Liberal regime pre-1922? If there are parallels, does this affect our analysis of the achievements, failures, and weaknesses of the Liberal regime?

Chronological Table

Domestic Events	Foreign Affairs
1870 Rome seized – unification complete.	
1871 Pope rejects the new Italian state.	
1876 Era of Depretis as prime minister begins.	
1877 Primary education compulsory.	
1881 Electoral reform adds two million voters.	
1882	Italy in Triple Alliance.
1883 Mussolini born.	
1885	Italy begins expansion in Eritrea and Somaliland.
1887 Death of Depretis. Crispi dominant political figure.	
1888 Tariff war with France begins seven years of economic depression.	
1891 Pope relaxes catholic ban on political activity with his *Rerum Novarum*.	
1893 Banca Romana scandal. Fasci emerges in Sicily.	
1894 Crackdown on Fasci and Socialists.	
1895 Socialist party (PSI) formally set up.	
1896 Fall of Crispi.	Italy defeated in Ethiopia.
1898 Widespread food riots. Massive emigration from south to the Americas begins.	
1899 Start of decade of economic growth. Fiat founded.	
1903 Era of Giolitti begins.	
1909 PSI poll 20 per cent of votes cast.	
1911	War in Libya.
1912 Universal manhood suffrage.	
1914 Giolitti resigns.	The First World War begins – Italy neutral.
1915	Italy enters the First World War.
1917	Italian defeat at Caporetto.
1918	End of the First World War – Italian victory.
1919 January, Catholic party (PPI) founded. March, Mussolini founds Fascist movement.	
	September, occupation of Fiume. September, peace treaty with Austria.
November, election makes PSI biggest single party in parliament.	
1920	peace treaty with Hungary.
September, occupation of factories. Winter, Fascist *squadrismo* takes off.	
1921 May, Fascist's electoral alliance with Giolitti gives them 35 seats.	

October, Mussolini creates the Fascist party (PNF) to cement his control over the movement.

1922 Winter/Spring, increased Fascist violence.
Summer, Fascist violence at peak.
August, Socialist general strike fails.
October, March on Rome. Mussolini appointed Prime Minister.
December, creation of Grand Council of Fascism.

1923 January, Fascist militia formed from squads.
Corfu incident.
November, electoral law passed.

1924 April, general election gives Fascists a majority in parliament.
Yugoslavia cedes Fiume to Italy.
June, murder of Matteotti followed by Aventine secession.

1925 January, Mussolini declares his intention to introduce dictatorial rule.
May, *Dopolavoro* created.
Locarno Treaties.
October, Vidoni pact bans free trade unions.
December, opposition parties banned.

1926 ONB youth organisation created.
Treaty of Friendship with Albania.
Ministry of Corporations set up – start of corporate state experiment.

1927 Launch of Battle for Births.
Treaty of Friendship with Hungary.
Revaluation of currency.

1928
Italy signs Kellogg-Briand Pact banning war.

1929 Lateran Agreement with Church.

1933 Institute for Industrial Reconstruction set up – state tries to alleviate economic depression.
Hitler comes to power.

1934
Italian troops sent to Austrian border to stop possible *Anschluss*.

1935 Mussolini increases drive for economic autarky.
March, Stresa Front.
October, invasion of Ethiopia.

1936
Rome-Berlin Axis formed.
Start of Spanish Civil War.

1937
Italy joins Anti-Comintern Pact.

1938
March, Austro-German *Anschluss*.
November, anti-Jewish laws.
September, Munich conference.

1939
March, Nazis seize Czechoslovakia.
April, Italy invades Albania.
May, Pact of Steel with Germany.
September, start of the Second World War – Italy 'non-belligerent'.

1940
June, Italy enters war.
September, attacks Egypt.
October, attacks Greece.
November, naval defeat at Taranto.

1941
April, loss of Italian empire in East Africa.

1943   July, Allies invade Sicily.
        26 July, Mussolini dismissed from
            office by the king.
        3 September, Italy signs armistice with
            the Allies.
        12 September, German troops rescue
            Mussolini from government prison.
September 1943–April 1945, Civil war in
    German-occupied northern Italy.
1945   April, end of war in Italy.
        28 April, execution of Mussolini.

Further Reading

A large number of books have been written about Italian Fascism but the Liberal period after 1870 has attracted much less attention. The following suggestions for further reading reflect this fact. The books recommended are readable and should be available in most public libraries.

M. Clark, *Modern Italy 1871–1982*, (Longman 1984)

This is the best up-to-date survey of the period. It looks not only at Italian politics but also at social and economic changes. Chapter 10 on the death of Liberal Italy and chapter 13 on the economy and society under Fascism are particularly useful.

D. Mack Smith, *Italy, A Modern History*, (University of Michigan 1959); *Mussolini*, (Granada 1983); *Mussolini's Roman Empire*, (Longman 1976); and *Italy and its Monarchy*, (Yale University Press 1989)

Mack Smith is probably the most prominent English-speaking historian of modern Italy and his work is always worth reading. His general survey, *Italy, A Modern History*, provides a very detailed account of the Liberal administrations after 1870 and is good on the period 1915–25 (pages 307–86). His biography of Mussolini, available in paperback, is well worth buying. It is excellent on his personality and on the political style of the Fascist regime. The remaining two books detailed above consider Fascist foreign policy and the relations between Italian governments and the monarchy respectively.

E.R. Tannenbaum, *Fascism in Italy – Society and Culture 1922–45*, (Allen Lane 1972)

Chapter 4 provides interesting insights on the Fascist economy, while chapter 5 is good on the ONB, *Dopolavoro*, and anti-Fascist dissent.

M. Knox, *Mussolini Unleashed 1939–41*, (CUP 1982)

Knox provides a fascinating interpretation of Fascist foreign policy, stressing Mussolini's aggressive instincts and bloodthirstiness. It also analyses the reasons for Italy's poor performance in the Second World War. Chapter 1 and the conclusion provide a brief summary of Knox's arguments.

A. Lyttelton, *Seizure of Power – Fascism in Italy 1919–29*, (Weidenfeld and Nicolson 1973)

The introduction covers the historiography of the period, while chapter 1 is interesting on the crisis of the Liberal regime.

123456789101112131415161718192021222324252627282930

C. Seton-Watson, *Italy from Liberalism to Fascism 1870–1925,* (Methuen 1967)

To increase your understanding of Italian politics and society at the beginning of our period it is well worth reading the prologue and chapter 1.

Acknowledgements

The publishers would like to thank the following for permission to reproduce copyright illustrations:

Topham cover; p. 74; Hulton Picture Company p. 75; Popperfoto p. 76; p. 77; David Low, Evening Standard/Centre for the Study of Cartoons and Caricature University of Kent at Canterbury p. 123.

Glossary

Anschluss	union of Germany and Austria in 1938.
autarky	economic self-sufficiency – Mussolini made efforts to achieve this in Italy after 1934–5.
autostrada	motorways.
Avanti	socialist newspaper edited by Mussolini 1912–14.
Banca Romana	financial scandal of 1893 involving prominent Liberal politicians.
Banco Ambrosiano	Bank involved in 1980s financial scandal.
Blitzkrieg	'Lightning war' – Nazi military doctrine.
Caudillo	title assumed by General Franco in Spain, meaning leader.
Confindustria	Italian employers' organisation.
coup d'etat	armed takeover of the state.
Das Kapital	Karl Marx's analysis of history and capitalist society. A fundamental text for Marxists/Communists.
Dopolavoro	Fascist organisation designed to control adults' leisure time. Organised sports, theatre, music, libraries, and night classes.
Duce	title assumed by Mussolini, meaning leader.
Fasci	protest movement in Sicily 1893–4.
Fasci di Combattimento	literally 'combat group', the movement founded by Mussolini in 1919 and known more commonly as Fascism.
Fascismo	Fascism.
Führer	Adolf Hitler's title – leader of Germany.
Latifundia	great landed estates, principally in the south, employing landless labourers usually on poor wages.
Legge Fascistissime	law of December 1925 banning political opposition.
Luftwaffe	German airforce.
Mein Kampf	Hitler's book describing his beliefs and intentions.
Opera Nazionale Balilla	Fascist youth movement designed to instil loyalty, obedience and martial spirit.
partisans	anti-Fascist resistance fighters active in German-occupied Italy 1943–5.

Partito Nazionale Fascista	official Fascist party formed by Mussolini in 1921 to cement his control over the Fascist movement.
Partito Socialista Italia	Socialist party established in 1895.
Podestas	appointed by the Fascist central government, these officials replaced town councils and elected mayors.
Popolari	Catholic political party, the PPI, founded in 1919.
Popolo d'Italia	newspaper established by Mussolini in 1914. Became the official mouthpiece of Fascism.
putsch	armed attempt to seize power, eg. Hitler's putsch in Munich in 1923.
ras	Fascist leaders in the provinces commanding their own squads of Fascists.
Rerum Novarum	statement issued by the Pope in 1891 indicating that the Church was prepared to consider the participation of catholics in Italian politics.
Risorgimento	Italian national and cultural revival of the eighteenth and nineteenth centuries, culminating in Italian political unification.
squadrismo	name given to campaigns of violence and intimidation carried out by Fascist gangs. Usually directed against socialists and trade unionists.
trasformismo	process of bringing together political groups of differing political persuasions in order to form a viable government. A policy employed extensively by Liberal politicians 1871–1922.
Untermenschen	Nazi term, meaning sub-humans, applied to Jews and slavs in particular.

Index

Abyssinia, *see* Ethiopia
Acerbo Law 64
Adowa, battle of 27
Albania 118, 127
Anti-Comintern Pact 125
anti-semitism 90
Austria 119–20
autarky 111
Avanti 28, 47
Aventine secession 65

Badoglio, Marshal 132–3
Balbo, Italo 50, 54, 82
Banca Romana 25
Battle for Births 106
Battle for Grain 102, 111

Catholic Church 16–17, 28–9,
    103–6
Christian Democracy 140–2
Confindustria 63, 111
Corfu Incident 117
Corporate state 101
Crispi, Francesco 24–7, 116
Cult of Personality 74–7

D'Annunzio, Gabriele 46
De Gasperi 141
De Stefani 98–9
Depretis, Agostino 22–4
dictatorship ch 4–5
Dopolavoro 108–10

economy ch 2, 3, 6, 7, 8
education 107
Emilia-Romagna 49–50
Ethiopia, war in 26–7, 121–4

Farinacci, Roberto 54, 82, 132,
    140
Fasci 25–6
Fasci de Combattimento 47–8

Fascism ch 3–7
Fiume 45, 46, 117
Franco, comparison with
    Mussolini 91–4

Garibaldi 16
Giolitti 21, 30–4, 35, 49, 51–2,
    65
Grandi, Dino 50, 54, 82

Hitler, comparison with
    Mussolini 84–91
  foreign policy ch 7

IRI 99

Kellogg-Briand pact 118–19

land reclamation 102
Lateran Agreement 104–5
Legge Fascistissime 66
Liberalism ch 2–4
Libya, war in 33
Locarno Treaties 118

Matteotti 65
Mussolini, early life and beliefs
    46–7
  founds Fascism 47
  rise to power 48–58
  creates dictatorship 4–5
  personal rule ch 5
  economy and society ch 6
  foreign policy ch 7
  death of 3–4
mutilated victory 45–6

Nationalists 32–5, ch 3

ONB 108
OVRA 83

Pact of Steel   127–8
Popolari   35, 48–9, 52, 63, 68–9,
   140
Popolo d'Italia   47, 48, 67, 132

Rome-Berlin Axis   124–5
Rome – March on   55–8
Roselli, Carlo   83

Socialism   27–8, 44–5, 54–7, 68
Spain, comparison with Italy
   91–4
Squadrismo   50–1, 80–1

Stresa Front   120

Trasformismo   22–4, 32–3
Triple Alliance   23, 42

Victor Emmanuel II   7, 15
Victor Emmanuel III   56–8, 73,
   78

World War, First   42–3
World War, Second   130–7

Yugoslavia   118